Moving to the Edge of the World

Moving to the Edge of the World

A Poetry Trilogy

Alla Renée Bozarth

Writers Club Press
San Jose New York Lincoln Shanghai

Moving to the Edge of the World
A Poetry Trilogy

All Rights Reserved © 2000 by Alla Renée Bozarth

No part of this book may be reproduced or transmitted in any form or by any means, graphic, electronic, or mechanical, including photocopying, recording, taping, or by any information storage retrieval system, without the permission in writing from the publisher.

Writers Club Press
an imprint of iUniverse.com, Inc.

For information address:
iUniverse.com, Inc.
5220 S 16th, Ste. 200
Lincoln, NE 68512
www.iuniverse.com

Cover design by Susan Lind-Kanne

ISBN: 0-595-16063-8

Printed in the United States of America

Acknowledgements

Various poems in *Moving to the Edge of the World* can be found in the following books and audiotapes by Alla Renée Bozarth:

Books

Gynergy
In the Name of the Bee & the Bear & the Butterfly
Sparrow Songs
Womanpriest
Life is Goodbye/Life is Hello
Stars in Your Bones
At the Foot of the Mountain
Soulfire

Audiotapes

Water Women
Reading Out Loud to God

Contents

Part One: Medicine Bear

Where Life Begins 3
A Visit Home for Christmas Rites 5
Jewels 7
Writing in a Foreign Language 9
Homecoming 10
Piscean Moon 14
Chinook 15
Salmon Return 16
Narwhal 19
How Can We Survive Our Choices? 21
What We Can Bear 22
An Ant 23
Going Formal 25
Cat's Act 26
Betrayal 28
Winter Trio 31
A Pig's Winter 34
Retreat 35
New Depth 37
Why I Came to the Country or Persephone Goes West 38
Waiting 41

Fear	43
Spiral Rest	44
Phaedrus Pool	45
A Second Coming	51
Oxbow Farm Incident	54
River Blindness	61
An Act of Love	63
Dzoónokwa	65
Sky Burial	66
What Is It?	68
Cross	69
Hunter	71
Verdi	73
I Am Your Poem	74
More Words for William Stafford	76
A Poem Heard	78
My Yoga Teacher	81
Country Cousins	83
The Amber Bears	84
Bear Hug	86
Innkeeper	87
On the Road Again	88
Coyote	90
From Here	92
Time Traveler	94
Reconciliation	96
Medicine Bear	98
Chrysalis	100
Biodance	102
Flying at Sixty Below Zero	104
Sea Flight	105
Hermes	106

Inanna in Hell	108
Destiny	110
Out from the Islands off North Carolina	112
In the Name of the Bee & the Bear & the Butterfly	113
Sometimes I Feel the Sky	117
Shaking	119
In Fields of Blue Lupine	121
Just the Right Tilt	122
A Surprising Species	124

Part Two: Burning Bush

Lost and Found	129
Volcano	130
The Elements Are in Charge	131
Burning Bush	132
Arctic Quest	134
The Blackbird's Child	136
Sabbath Light	140
Not an Ordinary Craziness but Reality	142
No Such Thing	143
Brown Dwarf	144
Ten Things I Do Not Understand	146
The Way Things Are	148
Greening Game	149
A Gathering of Poets at the Lan Ting Pavillion in 353 C.E.	151
Literary Ecology	152
Owl	153
Turn	155
At the End of this Road	157
White Train	159

Plumed Serpent	161
Taquitz	163
The Wood that Hides	166
Cosmic Eye-con	168
Rachmaninoff Weather	169
The Legend	170
Winter Dream	174
The Cutting	177
Things Get Broken	180
How an Old Ojibwa Man Became a Priest	181
Fire of the Earth	183
Gloria	186
Tree People	187
Redemption	188
God Is a Verb	189
Prayer Dance	191
Easter Bear	192
Christ	193
Vigil	194
Moonbath Conception	196
Celebration	198
Music	200
Eclipse	201
Seven Peaches Jar	203
My Body the Earth	205
Cape Foulweather	206
And I Walk Among Them	209
"Do You Live Alone?"	211
On Being a Mammal	214
Easter Gatha	217
Hymn to Gaea	218

Part Three: Eaten by Angels

Colors Derive 221
Blessing of the Stew Pot 223
Creature Covenant 225
Seeing the Cellist 227
Nagwalagwatsi 229
Bakerwoman God 230
Country Life 232
On Killing a Recluse Spider 236
Quail 238
Conscientious Objection 240
My Feet Press Flowers 242
Dinner at the Alexis Esplanade 243
My Place 244
After the Tempest 246
Revenant 248
Holding Together 250
Seasoning 252
Tending 253
August Apples 254
Peaches on the Counter 256
Sun Singer 257
Sparrow 259
Fall Quartet 260
    Sun Jeweler 260
    Red 260
    Falling 260
    Cosmic Child 261
Windowscape 262
All Saints Morning/All Souls Eve 263
Playing with Angels 265

Real Presences—Nightbird 267
Horowitz to Tea 269
Freedom 271
Banshee 272
Piston's Suite from *The Incredible Flutist* 275
Why I Wear Black 277
Blackbird 278
The Swan 279
Crow 281
Something More 283
Requiem and Kaddish 285
Under the Ironwood Tree 287
How Hard for a Mother or Father to Let Go of a Son or Daughter 291
Christmas Morning Mass 294
Pleiades' Daughter 296
Fantaisie-Impromptu 299
When Poets Kiss 301
Three-handed Solitaire 303
You Angels Who Cluster 305
What Am I Doing? 307
Cycles 309
"What is Prayer?" 311

Part One

Medicine Bear

Where Life Begins

not in tidal pools but
in the thermal vents between
Earth's shifting plates in
the Ring of Fire—the Mountain below

The urges of Earth
are there:
in the hot, hidden
down-under places

between worlds
where surface meets
surface and melts
in the opening.

This, then, is
the cosmic kiss
where all that
is hard touches
its own Other,
transforms
enticingly,
consummates
and makes
the Never-before.

Where no sun gives light,
no micron escapes
the Divine Fire
from Within, surging
and frothing to come forth

and secret clay
crystals merge
and marry
in such wet heat
of Meeting.

This is where
Life Begins
then:
neither here nor there,
but all ways Between.

A Visit Home for Christmas Rites

I drive myself home from the airport
with Mother to meet me.
It is the third time this has happened,
this visit to the stranger I was,
what the mind clings to as home.

The familiar constantly recedes
(some of us accept this).
The fog is extraordinary,
an extraordinary space of nothingness
hovering palpably above us.
We have been trained to ascend
(the emptiness of height
should be no surprise).

A strange sensation to drive in fog,
the white lines on both sides
disappearing into infinity.
Two red eyes ahead outreach
one's ability to see
and then there is only the void.

The animal coming from the left
has countless procession of eyes
penetrating the night.
This takes immensity of hope.

Our destination is behind us.
We pray to our past for release
and a new way to find each other.
We huddle in a cult of candles
and atavistic song for New Year's light.

Out of our holy yearning we give
(we were not taught to receive).
Time is running out for giving.
We give to emphasize our living.

Jewels

Mama gave this shimmering
bracelet to me one New Year's Eve
and we danced the new year in
together. I was eighteen.
That same year I wore it
all over Europe traveling
with her.
Winging my wrist I danced
with the Flamenco dancer
in Madrid's largest nightclub
after he gallantly bowed
to ask my mother's permission.
I wore it watching underwater
nude ballet at the Moulin Rouge,
and to the opera with Mama's
elegant Russian cousin after
the night Orient Express
from Vienna to Hamburg.
And when the Greek sea captain
proposed to me at dawn after
watching me sleep in my mother's
lap all night from Verona to Rome
on another train from the Cote d'Azure.
Years later, the year I married
and my mother died, I lost it.

Eighteen Easters passed since then,
and it's reappeared, with one missing stone;
I take it as a tribute in crystal economy
of the cumulative losses I've known—mother,
father, husband, home, work, and world—
from time to time through intervals of grace.
I keep this gift in my jewelbox now,
bracing myself against old age and widowhood.

But once a year at midnight on New Year's Eve
I shall wear feathers and silk, with friends
or alone, and the gleaming bracelet, too,
pull out all the stops and let myself shimmer
in refashioned glory, an orgy of memory
and hope even the old can afford.

Writing in a Foreign Language

> I have always felt that prose
> was my second language.

Women before me and my time
were forbidden access to books,
whether reading or writing,
learning—even the language
of learning, tongue of the gods.
Hebrew, Arabic, Latin, Greek—
forbidden.

Gifted women hold your tongues.
Keep silent before man
and let him play the fool
alone in costly parody.
When the world is sick enough
will be your time to speak
and write in golden letters
the ancient wisdom words
of healing power, the natural
voice of the Mother Tongue.

Homecoming

Those fish are not the only
animals driven home by death.

I too have been at sea,
a deep sea swimmer.

I too have grown
red-fleshed and thin-

blooded
in my journey.

An inland ocean's holding,
submerged in duty, learning,

diving off the edge of inner
ridges unrelenting and on fire,

seeing miracles
at the Source.

I too know my inkling times
and their span.

Eons verge symmetrically.
In no time, the time of return.

At first no hint
of failing,

the waning breath
and defiant

leap
of two-thirds free.

All changed.
Time burned out of me.

Silver-skinned,
half turned to salt,

I start the end,
all atoms urging.

The Dance begins.
We turn and turn again

in unison,
bones and happy molecules

and the compact
organs singing:

Out of the depths
to the rivers, and light.

I am coming
to the hard and gentle place

for the Great Marriage
to propagate my Kind.

I am becoming
the river and light

in my longing,
I am metamorphic,

a living seaplane
in my dreams,

fins unfolding
into wings.

I am a living
seaflower

climbing rivermountains
impossibly.

My labor toward death
is Original Play.

I remember
this struggle

is how I was born,
came to be.

My scaly petals cover, kiss
my sisters' eggs in passing.

My pink blood blesses, greets
tomorrow, fades gratefully

into another body.

Piscean Moon

Salmon gleam
rose red one mile
far & deep at sea—
seagulls glimmer
silvershimmer on
sleeping rocks
near shore—
beyond shining
amethyst sand
a fiery apricot
full moon resting
on black water.

Chinook

So near my goal
an impossible weight
presses down, stresses
and shapes to deform.
My tortured body
twists into the current
and now ten million tons
of water come down
upon me, all heavy,
all is heavy, all slowed
to an imponderable wait
so near to home.
Did you bring me over
the threshold to die?

Salmon Return

Do not plant me
in too-high lakes
and leave me to die,

climbing against the current
never to take nourishment
again, damaged by men's nets,
determined, determined
to go home.

I risk all,
lose all.

From too-shallow basins
I fly up waterwalls,
become breakfast for bears,
foxes, seagulls, my children
magpies' supper,

am pushed through false tunnels
up metal ladders, frightened
all the way.

Survive. Survive.

Five years at sea,
then I track my way
through the impossible,
journey to thrive
in a few hours' ecstasy
when I live only to love,
then die with my mate
content in five days.

My body transforms for this,
red and round with roe,
my face an obsessive mask,
teeth tortured upward
with one purpose under stars:
home. Home.

In my final waters
at the top of the world
my faithful mate and I
prepare to dance and die.

Together we rise along rocks,
ripe for love, past beached
friends too weak for this orgy
of fulfilling glory.

Now the last brief fall Up,
my life-battered body too weary
for this small step at the end.
My children! My love!

Bring me home!
Strength for this journey!
Oh! breath still in me,
let me leap!

Narwhal

Does the narwhal
sing like its gentle
cousin, killer whale,
remembering lullabies
for children under ice?

Does it play,
remembering human days
millennia ago,
sea unicorn of the Deep?

Does it leap and cavort
like the southern penguins
rock-hopping for fun?

Does it die
humming in its blood,
where harpoons suck
for oil, men pull
its proud tusk out
for gold?

Or does it lie
about at bottom,
sea bear of the north,
snoring through its horn,

until it tops itself
to breathe a bit of spring?

Forgotten beast, stay hidden.
Play down below and never
let men see you.
Be our hero, not our victim.
Be mysterious, be our fantasy,
but be safe.

How Can We Survive Our Choices?

The main thing is
to lead one's life,
not let it happen.

Life's a choice
and also a gift
to be enjoyed.

Experience experience!
Immerse yourself in it!
Revel in the breathing
bubbles of it!

To go in the path
of one's innermost choice,
the essential thing is
to listen to one's dreams
a little more than
to one's friends.

Otherwise, the ghosts
of friends may leave us
alone when we are dead,
to face without solace
the ghosts of our murdered dreams!

What We Can Bear

Earth's electrolytes
dazzle in silence
the quiet minutes
past dawn, the still
mirror of twilight water
when shorebirds cease
to graze and simply look,
when joggers stop
beating the motherbreast
and listen for an instant
to her heart, when the pansy
pants for light,
and the violet thirsts
for violent downpour
of waterfall
but knows enough
to hold her breath instead.

An Ant

An ant
crawls bravely
around & around
the periphery
of the rearview mirror
grasping the edge
trying various angles
of exit
to no avail—then it is not
an ant but most musical
three-part bug, orange or
Chinese red at the head and
thorax, a gracefully scalloped
black and white pelvis with
a valentine tip for tail;
with its antennae it sniffs
at plastic & steel, its six
legs circumferencing
the rectangular flatness—
to help it out or watch breathless,
hoping it will figure it out
for itself, with the aid of some
ionic vibration of encouragement—
jump! or if the heart on your tail
is hidden wings enfolded, fly!
take off! no.

back forth up down around
Flick. Now it proves it can
skate perfectly vertically on
sheer glass. Can it see itself?
Finally the human impulse to interfere—
an impatient but tender kleenex lifts
the thing from its small reflexive
universe & shakes it to cement.
Was it right, or well done?
How vulnerable the horizontal
bent of the pavement,
how flat & unseeing
the soles of shoes!

Going Formal

zebras
penguins
puffins
pandas

buffleheads
ring-necked swans
snow leopards

black-eyed polar bears
white-browed blackbirds

Nature loves
her black and white
ties and tales

Cat's Act

A huge winter white cat
is straddling along the length
of my redwood fence,
considering descent
into snow.

Will it jump?
It resists, hesitates,
walks on, stops, considers,
resumes.

Finally,
as I wait
for the Moment
of white on white,

the cat refuses to plunge
and simply walks, upside down,
to the cold blanket below.

I do not see
the moment of contact,
hidden by shrubs.
Only the cat's fur
swaying smugly
from side to side

in self-satisfied ripples
as it strolls off
behind the tool shed,
as if to tea
with gloves on all fours.

Betrayal

We cats prowl
at night
when everyone
else on our street
is decently in bed
pretending to be sane
and having disturbed dreams.

We walk through our dreams
under blue streetlamps,
up and down in the glare
of auto-mobiles, away
from the dead end
where we've come to live.

Undirected and undressed
in a shock-
ing thin night-
gown and gold-
en slip-
ers not meant
for mount-
ain climbing
or descent
on rough
pavement,

the hair-
dresser's mis-
take suits me
wonder-
fully, makes
us kin: my head-
fur black and electric—
look, the contrast
of white skin,
the echoing black
and white bulge
of accusative eye!

No diurnal deception now.
Night reveals all:
the inner world and
the universal affinities,
heavenly bodies over-
coming the soul's solitude.

By day we fool
our households:
they think we're domestic.
It's when we meet in the
middle of the moon's turn
here in the dark,
bowing to each
other's shadow,
claws stretched
out, teeth bared,
that we see

and revel
in the true
wildness each inner
animal knows best
of itself,
awake under stars
and in heat,
Yowling and Howling
and holding
daylight at bay!

Winter Trio

Violin I

Before the winter-watch
observe how leaves
love gravity, birds
flying to earth
in circles.

Each bird makes down up,
finds safety in a nest of sod.

Chestnuts, old apples, rinds rotting
soften Earth into her hard, cold sleep.

Under feathers of snow she digests them.
Each spring, new eggs crack, branches get wings,
each leaf a resurrected god.

Piano

In the winter, wait
for words. Keep clean.
Do normal things.
Care for the body.
Keep one ear to the ground

to hear the whir of Earth
turning. Notice any dizziness.
Keep one nostril open, alert
to telling changes in air moisture
or Earth odor;
catch nature mixing
her metaphors, defying certain rules.
Notice the wetness of stones.
How tender the pear skins.
Pungent the flesh down under.
Look for dark spots on the fingertips
to tell you when the blood is ready.
And when hair flies upward from the ears,
electric, it is time.
Settle in with tea in a blue violet cup.
Turn off electricity. Light candles. Cocoon.
Oil the skin. Take pen. Write
the awkward Begin: how fast/slow/ spin.
A baby hiccuping into life.

Sigh yourself awake. Laugh a little. Shake.
Breathe.
Later, tears for thanks.

Interlude for Cello

Bears are born in caves
in winter while their mothers
sleep.

Below glistening ice

in the deep crystal cave
the feel of underwater,
of fluid air and shimmering
space: She emerges swimming
awake, the Great One,
licks light from her salt walls,
nurses, rises at the opening,
a paw lifted—
Watch.
Under a milky moon
the hunter approaches, unarmed,
forgetting whose death his mission is,
sees his own, stunned, speaks
the secret words the Dreamer cannot
bring back, receives not the expected
attack but only the silver bear's blessing,
is tamed by the beast.

Violin II

    My winter-wait
    like the small death
    of Night
    turns, horns of the moon
    from right hand to left,
    until, unblinded,
    I see the crocus
    coming green through ice,
    find again the courage
    to speak.

A Pig's Winter

A pig's winter bedded
we slid on snow shoes
down the furious slope
to find them
there a yard
from our car,
barned up last night
we came at noonrise.
Now out, they're running
scared, their furry ears
catch our step,
we, startled to see them,
grunt, give a laugh,
run high with the still
bare track slide,
our furs on end
admiring them,
the three great
tan-furred
pigs.

Retreat

Through lost treble and low
moaning branches motorsounds
invade the snowstunned farm.
(Buddhists could transcend
samsara here, Hindus forget
the necessities of bhakti,
Christians reach the prayer of quiet,
all persons run from or meet themselves.)

Northwest of the city the half-plowed road
turning to a track, then to a trail,
past two yellow warning posts:
      No trespassers
      Pine Valley Farms
Trout fishing in summer,
twelve hundred acres owned for the right
to fish in Sand Creek, a club
of casters and reelers.
We escape here at deep year's end,
solitary, our meditative healing,
renewing, uniting three days.

The caretakers reach the barn
and gate, follow the fence
with their clean new truck,
then noiseless as their care

violate the property with shovels,
gone to dig a grave.

New Depth

The soul
when left
out in
the cold
tends
to lose
its voice
which
once
it returns
speaks
from a new
depth.

Why I Came to the Country or Persephone Goes West

The whole venture
is embarrassing.

Kissing my friends Goodbye
I mutter "I wish I knew
what I was doing…"

I have to go there.
I want to go there.
And I am loathe to go.

The drive across mountains
through deserts, finally
following the River home.

A naked season.
All the tree-bones exposed.
Browned Earth. Underground
pipes burst; aerial antenna bent,
toolshed blown down
in the Christmas storm.
Garbage strewn about.
The gate to the field
wide open.

This is what
greets me.

I want to tear up
the grape vines that last
summer choked my cherry trees,
I want to grab their dry tendrils
and send them packing.
I want to cut down the pampass grass
before it comes to the door demanding meat.
I want to plant roses—lots of them.

Instead, I leave the debris
for the insurance man,
scoop up armloads of rotten leaves
from the porch into plastic bags,
rake out the pond, wash windows
between storms, ponder futility
in all forms, bake muffins to keep warm,
keep the stewpot going for hearty smells,
count cars on the gravel road,
order new curtains,
visit the neighbors,
drink gallons of tea,
stay in bed,
listen to the wind,
think I hear wolves
howling at night,
find my own grief,
begin to feel it fully,
keep my skin wet,
let red sweat drop

on the paper,
and wait wait wait
for something new to happen.

Waiting

for the Eschaton: Minnesota Poem

I am waiting for winter to be over
I am waiting for the headache to stop
I am waiting for the board meeting to end
I am waiting for poetry to save me
I am waiting to go home
I am waiting to find courage
I am waiting to have enough time
I am waiting to be rested
I am waiting for my vision to improve
I am waiting for morning
I am waiting for night to come
I am waiting for sleep
I am waiting for sunshine
I am waiting for warm weather
I am waiting for first snow
I am waiting to grow up
I am waiting for the reassuring flow
I am waiting for the cessation of flow
I am waiting for the birth pains
I am waiting for the birth pains to end
I am waiting for children
I am waiting for children to grow up
I am waiting for menopause
I am waiting for grandchildren

I am waiting for work
I am waiting for retirement
I am waiting for a vacation
I am waiting for the vernal equinox
I am waiting for Easter
I am waiting for summer solstice
I am waiting for the bus
I am waiting for the airplane
I am waiting for the telephone to ring
I am waiting for the telephone to stop ringing
I am waiting for school to start
I am waiting for school to be over
I am waiting for Christmas
I am waiting to stop defining myself by the things
for which I wait
I am waiting for this poem to begin
I am waiting for my death
I am waiting to know what to do
I am waiting to do nothing
I am waiting to be young again
I am waiting for ever
I am waiting

Fear

fear that the gas stove will blow up
    & destroy me before my dinner is done

fear that I will lose control of my car

fear that I will fall off the wing of the airplane
    attempting to escape from flames of a crash

fear that I will be raped in an elevator

fear that I'll be struck by lightning
    & electrocuted while taking a shower
    during a storm

fear of being crushed & killed by the wait within

fear of the illusion of time

fear of cold

fear of snow

fear of telling too much truth in public

fear of making myself ill with fear

Spiral Rest

I am the Nautilus now
back in her shell, still,
on the ocean floor, true
to the dark, waiting…

Phaedrus Pool

1

Dappled streets losing ourselves in them
scurry our bewitched conveyance on.
One disaster on another.
No gas and a highwayman glaring
his lights at the children stuffed in the back.
Then just inside the Van Dusan Corridor on old Highway 18
at 2a.m. (coffee royal in our cheeks for warmth,
two thermoses to last the night) when determination
      nearly failed:
black ice on the road making visible each letter on the *To*
      Hebo sign
in asphalt transparency, burnt umber fog came in to conjure
our separate familiars against one another.

At the far stretch of our vision a deer leaped out
and in one blinded frenzy climbed over and under and over again
the grille and left wheel of the car, staggering and lunging
forward and up four feet in the sky in that completely honest
timidity that belongs to children before they learn the meaning
of doubt.

A bay-studded doe with enormous magenta eyes that soon
    glazed over,
a rippling body that gave happily to the merciful ax,
release from that awful irreprehensible fear.

When you pet a wild and dying animal
it emanates into your hand the perfect terror
of its own mortality, in the faithlessness anguish
peculiar to humans, around the steady fix of its eyes
two recesses of bestial praise, a sweat of homage,
a creaturely hymn through the loose pant of the lagging
    tongue.
Jackals and dogs would find her in the ditch and, eating away
literally at her open and alive heart, consuming the pulse
in her flesh while it throbbed most violently,
promote the regal death.

The ax fell with the full force of an avenging god.
The children did not see the blood pool flowing in the ravine.
We crawled out of our horror to tell them she ran safely back
into the forest where she would be happy
and wept in each other's arms.

2

By noon the next day the men had soldered the torn radiator
with acid and pepper for sediment.
We left the farmhouse
where the night and morning

passed,
thanked the old widow for breakfast
and drove on.

Delake is an hour-and-a-half from home.
Eventually it took us thirteen.
We wondered about a fine
and the state troopers
but it was too late now.

3

There it was, the ocean along Twenty Miracle Miles,
our womb, blessed mother, refuge, succor.
Resting on a kelp bed a single dead wrangly juniper
four meters beyond the front door, a totem pole
on the opposite side to ward off hungry sea nymphs
and small scavenger animals.
We had the oldest log cabin on the old crag of a hill,
rough as 1650 only the Indians gone; up a walled peak
in timbered rock and stone a bolted French door,
windows with tiny Swedish panels criss-crossed
making diamonds in the attic.
From these we peered out
on the bright phosphorous,
the lustful tide
coming in at midnight.

4

We rolled all through the incomprehensible hours
in the dark on our small straw cot in the loft,
cramped cozy, only the occasional raining of sweat
spilling between us.

The wood stove gave off too much heat most of which
ascended to the top corner where we slept.
We flew open the multi-colored window
to take in the water and whole expanse of the beach:
amber, rust, mustard, cobalt, turquoise and scarlet panes,
wind-worn cracks and shot holes, the slant roof
burying us against the galaxy.

A kerosene lantern hanging from the center crossbeam
and swaying in a draft forming fantastic shadows everywhere.
We felt like stowaway pirates in the hull of an ancient galleon,
the belly of an ocean angry around us, beating up
at the gunwales, isolated as only a ship and a sea
can be in midwinter.

Rain cymballing down on the cedar roof, driftwood tossed
on the sand like the amputated limbs of a sea god, breakers
crashing against the cliff and spray so high
we could taste it in our beds.
A little higher and the sky
was worth falling into.

5

We awakened to a strange shadow that scanned the length
of the horizon like a cross, great lights forming the crossbeam.
We thought it must be the ultimate passion and tomorrow

would be Paradise that would resurrect our bodies
from some conch shell long covered on the beach.

At daybreak the kids went down to collect rocks
and other fascinations.
Midmorning was dangerous for the riptide
began to play at human toes from too little distance,
so we snuggled them in for naps
and watched the treachery
of that lunar ensign alone together.

Washed up seaweed resembled giant carrots with ribbon tops.
A promontory sun hovered in the eastern sky
above the orange fog and tree swirled caves,
a column of spindrift.

The name you wrote last night
had become elongated.

Mara

in delicate transparency
that made my image
crest to the sea.

Mara Mara

the gulls cried after me.
I set off in a run.

The little sandpipers looked carelessly merry
riding the waves ducking in and out flying
catty-corner into the blanched jewel foam.

You watched me playing with them and allowed me that
      freedom.
I looked down the shore and suddenly there was a rock
      jutting out
the back of another rock and appeared the grace
of a prehistoric antler.

A deer leaped out on the water.

A Second Coming

1

When I was a child growing younger
(the natural process for those born old)
I remember a glistening spring morning,
shattered glass, sharpest splintering noise.

Five-thirty a. m. of a snowy end-of-March day,
shaken from sleep by the cry of wings on sand,
I followed the golden shadows of my dreaming,
found the living room dismembered, burning
with refractory dawn through a broken-open
eastern bay window.

Tables upturned, curtains swirling
by their own wrenched movement
on the floor, pierced, all chairs, chair, carpet,
wall, transfixed with infinitesimal window pane,
scattered by the daze of the stunned female pheasant
enthroned in grace on the velveteen couch.

Coarse, bitter and cold in the harshness life offered,
we looked at each other the loneliest moment of our
      lives,
while our unborn families slept through this meeting

in light.
Unusual winter air compelled her and them
to heavy sacrilege movement, out of stillness
where I was left desolate, alone in exquisite awe.

Thick blankets were placed
to keep out excess of light and cold
across the half-wall of space, rupturous.
In evening I inquired of our winged guest
and was told by Mother that the sheriff
had let her free where she burst out
with aim straight over the cemetery woods.

2

This evening of my ancient youth
the picture of a fated blue heron
brings the purple bright morning
of all my childhoods into a single eye:
images of my past on the unreal, visible
time track, the great bird
hopelessly tangled in itself
by human carelessness,
the heron's glass eye aimed up
toward a shattered sun.

My soul groans with the loves
it had no right to make.
On a light orange path
of just-before-autumn,

Grand River sunk in oil,
chemical debris, weighs
the heron's wings with death,
delivers her narrow determined
beak-head to innocent animal
joy whose mortal soul escapes,
flies homeward, as all my flaming
feathery hairs stretch
to the opening sky...

Oxbow Farm Incident

1

The only time in all my life
I stayed outside all night.
The man led me down
unseen gullies in the dark,
tripping on twigs, my legs
bleeding from blindness,
the cut of summer insects,
thistle, the jagged rock
I stumbled on falling
and rising in rhythm
with invisible small animals,
the flowers wild by day
tamed in the calyx of night.
I have no reason to be here.

We are supposed to be asleep.
The horses are asleep in the pasture.
It is too hot for the stables.
There is no reason to trust him,
but I don't let go of his hand,
am disturbed by my excitement
in not being able to see.

We are running, chasing heat
lightning coming in from the state
east of here.

We are not lovers, the man and I.
He is an Anglo professor of Chinese poetry.
In the dark we have discussed allomorphs
and phonemes and have had verbal climaxes
over isomorphs of the Li T'ai Po Period.
He is spectacled and gray-bearded and too thin.
Neither of us knows why we have felt compelled,
after two hours of this sitting on the damp earth
unable to see even our faces, to kiss each other
chastely on the lips, once only.
We are completely incongruous
and shall never see each other again.

He knows his brother's farm remarkably,
carefully leading us past danger, around
troughs, through beds of sleeping pigs.
We travel by dark of the moon.

2

No light but what the lightning gives.
Earlier constellations die to us or we to them
in the Arms of the Bear as August air
comes down with moist and manic vengeance.

Orange lightning,
peculiar fragments
cutting the night,
outraging a fury
inside us.

Soon we
will be
devoured.

3

It comes.
The sky has let forth
with demons.

Across a blank screen
in stereo, in menacing sync
they bolt,
upright,
sideways,
a flat sheet of foil
through the middle.

Locked in each others arms
for support on the earth
the man who is not my lover
and I are knocked to the forest floor,
cry out, shudder at the unhuman
sound we hear, rise

to our knees, run
before we come
to our senses, our soles
flying above ground,
the water now,

the sudden inscrutable water
comes crushing, comes crashing,
collapsing the air
between

our feet and the black
grass beneath.

We do not move
but are driven
forward.

Toward the farmhouse
where everyone else
faithfully sleeps.

We are the outlaws.

4

Looking sideways I see his eyes
have turned orange and are inverted triangles.
Has he become something unreal, a creature

of someone's insanity, of the running, a mad
emperor abducting me into his oriental nightmare?

We are far beyond words now.
My hand has melded into his.
My body has turned to liquid bronze.
I am one with the electric water.
He has made me fire-daughter!

This man who is not my lover
is no one I came here with.
He is the stranger
I have always known.

5

The horses.
The horses have awakened.
They are driving eastward.

The scream I hear
is no longer mine
or the man's,
but theirs.

We run with one rhythm,
running insanely in sync.
Our bodies gleam with onyx blue
of wet horsehair.
The mud has come to our knees.

We no longer breathe.
We who are all motion.

We are singing,
singing wild horse songs
and will never reach
the small white farmhouse.

We grow large, larger
than the house, stables, barn,
the white fields, our bodies
turned to strobe,
the fence between us
and the terror-stung beasts
rising higher and thinning,
taking to air

while we hear it,
hear the horse laughter
lift from the pit of the ground's
raw belly, hear the drumming
hooves covering our faces,
beating our eyes
and voices
down

into ground,
back into Earth,
driven beyond
animal song,

below grass,
by summer waters
without mercy,
our bodies

sound-shattered,
the rain
burning

down

inside us
all the way
to the rock—

River Blindness

First the thick black fly
comes up from the river,
seeks out and finds the most
virile flesh, takes its time,
then hones in for the bite,
leaving offspring behind.
Larvae grow there over
a lifetime, move through
the body just under the surface.

His family knew him always
as kind, good-hearted, quiet.
But even the gentle old man
has malice under the skin.
It manifests as irritation
first, then an evil laugh
and bent gleam in the eye,
and then the light goes out.
The worm climbs through
his skin, making its flame
mark and goes up to his eyes,
stealing sight and leaving
its own false light as trade
for vision.

The little boy leads
his grandfather through reeds,
wonders why the old man whose
touch like velvet soothed him
laughs outright when they pass
the smell of dry blood on bone,
keeping secrets, dark
in himself.

An Act of Love

The man thought
he was angry.
He was afraid.

The man thought
he was angry.
He was sad.

The man thought
he was angry.
He was unsure.

The man thought
he was angry.
He was lonely.

The man thought
he was angry.
He was lost.

The man thought
he was angry.
He was tired.

The man thought
he was angry.
He was confused.

The man thought
he was crazy.
He was alive.

    Then the man came to a place
    in the forest where a great tree
    had been split by lightning.
    He fell into its wound
    and let the tree hold him
    as he knelt with his arms
    clinging tight to the burnt bark.
    Filling its wound with his tears
    the man cried—

        "Oh, Tree, I've been
        hurt and burnt open
        just like you!"

Dzoónokwa

(Wild Woman—Kwakiutl)

Raven child
dried blood skin
wooden gold nose
cry-opened mouth
wildbeast eyes
brown like a bear's
crazed fairy hair
between two suns—
birthsun, deathsun—
Owl spoke her husband's name
fifty years too soon.

Sky Burial

Since the lamas left
no one's been well-
buried here.

All, like only the poor before,
thrown to the fish in the river,
a fisherman's gift to the gods
of the sea.

Gone a quarter century,
the illegal rites
past gold-leafed stupas
and smiling Buddhas,
the bodhisattva sutras
of Infinite Compassion,
forbidden.

Gone the freedom to believe aloud
in the old ways, when a single
portion of spittle could heal
the sick in the house of holy men.

But now only the Old Ways hold
life for the few still alive
in these marooned mountains.
Let them have their tea

tainted with syrup of sacred
yak butter, their offering of flowers
to the golden-winged dead,
their relative worship.

Let them die as they wish,
again call the lama-podebs
to yank the hair from the head
of the newborn dead
to insure clear passage.

Let the lama-jobas come
and clear the streets of the stench
of some cultural decay, carry
their corpses up to the mountain,
each day in the desert offer
a divine dinner to birds of prey.

Let the few trees left lift up
these ancestor bodies to disappear
utterly in the morning sky,
for Earth's dawn shines dimly
on human life, leaves little
cleansing fire from western ways
of death, leaves little ground left
in Earth's lap for cradle or grave.

What Is It?

The scream that follows
the artist into
the Vast Space
within bone

could it be
the sound
of creation

of many creations
creating each
cosmos from
void

and the sound
of the void
before

color
only
the empty
and open
soul

can know?

Cross

He crosses
the bridge
to meet
the Barefooted Archer.

She spent
ten years
making her bow.

Closing one eye
on the middle
of the bridge she
aimed into the shadows.

He saw nothing
on the other
shore—

Then he left
the old light,
ran after

her vision
into the void,
found her

bent over
the black feather
she shot.

No one saw
how she moved
off the bridge

entirely
to the other side.

Hunter

I am tracking
the vision,
recognize all
its signs
now.

As clear
as deertracks
or the awareness
of bear—I follow
the wildberry signs,

taste its scent
in the air,
know the trail
it leaves low
in the sky, sense
its larger winter
body.

I step carefully
around the waste
of the dream,
know what
it eats,
know

what it needs.

It needs me.
As I need the dream,
my dreamprey needs me.

Each other's prey,
each other's twin,
each other's secret,
each other's mate,
each other's own.

I am
at the edge
of my own
fatigue,
stand in the center
of the dream,
emptied.

Soon I will kill it,
I will make it come true.
Soon I will free it,
give birth to us both.

Verdi

Verdi, whose life
was music,
had no music
at his funeral.

Why do we always
seek some other
medium?

I grow to hate
words, wish also
for the medium
of silence (but
to remember the sound
of an avalanche
and ocean surf and
waterfalls and
rain), wonder

how it would be
to die, and dance
before I dream.

I Am Your Poem

Listen. I am your poem
and I feel sorry for you.
You are unimportant, merely
the poet, my conduit,
silver chalice made of clay,
but I want to tell you
I love you anyway, because
you let me live.
Even though you are weak
and foolish, full of many faults
and sometimes vain, you are
a good enough soul to let me through.
Your love is my matter, my living,
and your spirit my living-room.
Your passion the pen by which
I write myself with your blood.
So don't worry when you find
yourself outcast because of me,
begged by the market place
to betray me for prose.
You defy the capitalist lust
and are faithful to me,
and poor, an outsider.
And I am telling you now
Thank You for your loyalty,
your willingness to pay the price
that crazed bums and prophets pay,

of continuing true, with or without
an audience, a publisher, a proud
possession of critical praise,
a fat check in the mail.
You let me speak without
judging my voice, let my voice
override yours.
With only the reward
I bring you brushing against your skin
from the inside, fluttering
on your eyelids like a persistent moth
in your dreams, with what small secret
ecstasy you know when I move
through you in love
—it is enough.
You let me live.
And I bless you.

More Words for William Stafford

Your poems inspire
me, although
we are different.

You are the Quaker
of words, spare
in images, yet
penetrating from some
pre-dawn vision,
your solitary
centering-down.

I am the eastern rite Catholic
of verse, excessive, flamboyant,
all smells and icons and bells.

Your stark tending
is what I admire,
you the Zen farmer
of words, you get it
right from the ground,
shaken clear through,

while I am the Tantric
gospel singer cum
belly dancer.

Ours could be a fair exchange—
incense for bread,
truth for truth.

While you harvest
the meanings reverently,
trembling, not too serious,
a life-lover to the end,
I'd shout hallelujahs
and carry on beside you.

Then I'd listen to what
your methods teach,
and learn ecumenically:

the deep settle
into sheer being,
the deep agreeable sigh
into clear seeing—

    O may this seeing give light,
        May this being be filled with praise.

A Poem Heard

a poem heard
> is stuttered
>> in the ear
>>> that opens
>>>> at the heart,

the subtle
> stutter
>> that draws
>>> forth the hum of

the poem straight
> through
>> brain-

stem
> into
>> the central

nervous
> system
>> and then to the blood
>> and the great
>>> stereo heart.

    The ear in the heart amplifies
        the poem twice
          over,

sucking
    it deep into itself,

sending
    it out wide,
      worldfree

into eternity—

HEY, COUSIN BEAR!
    Hey, cousin bear!

For instance,
    so
      that

the felt music can
    filter
      through the left
      and right,

behind and before,
    bottom and top,
      all through

and the meaning
    can be
      an echo

    on the strings
        of the soul

    that will live
        in the body
        forever

My Yoga Teacher

We meet again
at the wire fence.
It is electric,
this artificial barrier,
but it allows me
to reach over or through
to touch you,
Sweet Pepper,
my neighbor, lovely
red cow,
to offer you cold, crisp
apples on a hot August day,
and gather up pears
that fell in a circle
under their trees.
These I throw and scatter,
unsure of your liking,
yet you come running
at the sound of your name,
willing to take my voice
as a sign
of offering, of peace
(I wish) between
our species, of friendship.

When I look into your eyes
and see myself, small,
and see you seeing me,
and feel the warm thick
roughness of your tongue
delicately licking my hand,
I grin with pleasure
and blush: forgive me
for taking so much from you,
human from cow.
You are an essential
presence in my daily
adoration.
You are beautiful.
I love you.
Thank you.

Country Cousins

Sing, Cousin Swallow,
Growl, Cousin Bear—

Go on about your being,
Wee Cousin Frog.

I want to open
the heart
of my ear
to your sound,
open my heart
to your song.

    Soorooo, Cousin Owl,
    Floorooo, Cousin Fish,
    Oohooo, Cousin Loon,
    ShooShooo, Cousin Moth,
    To you, Cousin Human.

        And the silence
        of the Tree
        and the stillness
        of the Sky
        and the Sound
        that They make
        when They meet.

The Amber Bears

In the wilder-
ness we saw them
such creatures you can't
imagine, wondrous
& enormous, three of them
with emerald eyes, not
ordinary orange bears but
the wild-
est grand things,
beautiful things, they
strode in on the backs
of fishes & sea lions,
they walked all night
upright for miles
to get here, come to us,
their fur matted with
blackberry juice,
with currant & boysenberry,
their mouths drunk with
amber honey, cinnamon
bears, ginger beasts
they come on & on, taller
than a building upright,
of caravan length, glorious,
beautiful things, their
paws lifted in exultation,

in praise, in greeting
of the day!

Bear Hug

The bears embrace,
hold tight with their
velveted paws
as if this
ursine hug would
prevent them
from falling off the planet.
They do not know
they have already fallen.
Waltzing in space
soon they will lick
stardust or seadust
from their faces
and be worried
that it tastes salty,
they will know they're in trouble
or at least in a different sort
of jam. Then one of them
will glance up and through
a diamond eye see the egg
poised above their heads
about to break, pregnant
with honey, essence
of amber, yolk of gold.

Innkeeper

No Lummi Indians left
on Lummi Island.
Now solo Fergus McCann,
the current resident,
recalls a native moon,
in respect with ancient
pride, takes small
bagpipes each evening,
paces out the arc
of shore, playing down
the sun.

On the Road Again

1

Under a prairie blood moon
in first quarter, entering
Scorpio the end of October,
crossing the length of North
Dakota: Kindred, Spiritwood,
and Bloom—
a perfect black cat, sleek
and small, jaguar fast,
runs across the interstate
freeway from nowhere,
just missing but not slowing
for the wheels of my rosered car
and the white one next to it—
Crystal Spring, Sweet Briar Lake
and Sterling Wing—
then nightfall, a dead white deer
on the grass.

2

Morning crosses eastern Montana.
Three magpies fly in front

of my moving window,
a black and white song.
I proceed westward against autumn wind,
blazing sun in my eyes for hours:
Custer, Big Timber, Pompey's Pillar.
Lewis and Clark led by Sacagawea,
who gave birth on the way,
invincible woman and guide, lover
of the ancient land who followed
her soul to the sea.
In the living stone I see her
features carved and moving,
a sun mirage to keep me
to the journey.

3

Just over the Yellowstone River
three black bomber jets dive up
out of nowhere, like Ringwraiths
from Middle Earth, Black Riders
of Mordor deprived of soul.
One ascends and crosses the path
before me, one over me, one after.
I shudder. All afternoon
across Montana I weep, aching
for ancient snowcrowned hills.

Coyote

Rough road trails through
Crazy Mountains into
the Beartooth Range.
I am autumn.
We follow the river
east, to greet the dawn-
sun.

Beside the road, your body,
Old Coyote, Trickster,
miracle-giver, birth-bestower,
time-keeper.

A truck hit you hard.
Your Spirit rose up, laughing,
howling with laughter.
I see patches of your calico fur
where your children buried you
in their mouths.

I see teethmarks on your long
and delicately pointed ears.
I see amber blaze on desert
oak trees.
I see green turning to blood
on leaves.

I see with your dark stone eyes,
Coyote.
Everywhere, I see where your Spirit went.

From Here

From here
the river
is a ribbon
of light—

One rose,
the color
of bright
coral seashell,
blooms
in the autumn
yard

and the pasture
grass dazzles green
with new rain
and low sun

and October trees
find their true
color again
before death—

From here
the waterfall

roars
below me

and the brave sun
smells cool.

From here the river
is a ribbon of light
and the full moon
rests a moment
abreast the red summit
of White Mountain.

From here I almost know
the secret of the stars,
how small the Earth is,
my own way home.

Time Traveler

My nemesis—no Greek goddess
but some medieval monk who first
conceived that clocks
were needed to call
men to prayer—and so
the beginning of dissociation
from the natural rhythms
of the heart toward God.

Ah, the mechanical hours,
then rude mechanicals,
the village clock towers
and the rule of the upright:
Be On Time!
But whose time?
Which long face to obey?
Two hundred to choose from
on the American frontier,
and chaos until the train
and telephone ushered in
the current system of splits:
time zones.

Benedictine time or Tellurian?
Cronos or Gaea?

From clock to computer
the commute's a disaster.
I'm back with the farmers
and free—from dawn to dusk
to live and work in the world,
then sleep and dream
with the moon and stars
and be always in time
with Earth's turn.

Reconciliation

Arab children have picked
hyacinth and cyclamen
for me from virgin beds
of the Olive Mount.

A Christmas gift
of Sharon and pieces
of fern with ochre twined
around tiny olive fingers.

These spring flowers
have come into my snow world
with the exact freshness and
surprise of the Incarnation,
at midnight, perhaps,
and in straw.

Made for love, my Lord,
Phoenix of the night,
tender and golden-throated,
feeding upon the lily,

O angel-winged, make
your flight into
the ashes of our hearts.

Bird of the morning
lighten our day,
rise singing
and be born!

Medicine Bear

They fly in secret,
without sound, blindly
sensing light.
Later, I find
their tiny corpses
circling the lamp,
or cradled inside
the ceiling globe.
They seem to have given
themselves wholly over
to light, its invisible
power.

ʊ ʊ ʊ

I fear suffocation,
walk in the sea
only to my knees,
never turn my back
on the horizon, guard
myself against glaring
noonday sun.

I want to know
where I am.

ಐ ಐ ಐ

The Bear is my totem.
Furclad, protected,
she sinks deep into
her body before
skin surface shows.
She cradles the dark,
worships at sunset.

Robust and large, she
tracks the moon when
it suits her, never
risking the regions
of fire.

In summer, noisy and open,
she feasts on wild blackberries
and trillium leaves, gorging
against winter's blinding
cold.

Later, in spring's first
February glimmer,
her cubs will drink near
to her skin, privileged
and warm, and savor
the sweet treasure
of wild blackberry milk.

Chrysalis

*I find myself
in the time between selves.
Transition*

I am pregnant with myself.
Do you realize what this means?
It means that every part of me
    must die,
all my cells and organs
    open and dissolve,
for I need their juicy substances
to nurture my new blood:
let teeth become eyes,
gullet become brain,
gray become bright red,
and hair turn into wings.
This is the truth of me—
I was, am, and shall be
    my Self, forever new,
        forever changed by changing,
creature blessed by consciousness,
    alive.

And this is not
a voiceless act, but a process
resounding inside death

with lusty shouts and whoops,
irregular and visible below
the carcass veil.
And death grows thinner,
giving way to God-knows-What—
diminishing like gauze
of spun sugar melting
in the sun.

Soon, I will be full-ripe
   with my Self,
able to nurse on sweet nectar,
free and light as living rain.
Soon, I will fly.

Biodance

everything bears the property of Love

Sitting on a rock in the Salmon River
watching first leaves fall.

From sunhigh mountain treetops
upstream the rapids carry
old branches to the sea,
their leaves landlocked already.

Why so soon?
Not soon at all—
your time is complete.
And so is mine.

You rest in sunlight
before transforming
into earth and air.

You dissolve your leafy form
and recompose into a thousand bodies.

Nothing ever ends.
Everything is always
   beginning.

Shall I find myself tomorrow
shining in a waterdrop

on a piece of moss
on the bark of a tree
that once was you?

Green into burntred,
old leaf, our biodance began
millennia ago, but today
I am glad to see you clearly
for the first time
with just these eyes,
my changing
partner!

Your bronze body
turns
to powder
with a crack
beneath my foot.

Part of you has already become me.
You are on your new way.

You will be back.
And so will I.
    So will I.

Flying at Sixty Below Zero

Who would have thought
the soft-looking smooth-sounding
clouds as hard as old mountains
ruptured out of sea rock
colder than deep night in space,
whiter than ice, the jet stream
my body makes on its solitary pathway home?

Crossing the great mountains before
the sea coast at the edge of the western world,
we plunge in our skyship heading toward
the crisp, cold, heady air of the eternal east,
chasing the sun halfway and
the snowsafe bluemarble Earth,
our bodies the communal infrared
furnace that gives all things life.

This space far above mountains
in chill sunlight, thinness of cloudlight,
clear beyond belief, beyond breath,
is only the way I go.
It is not, finally, home.

Sea Flight

Nightship
starship
giant gray whale
swimming in a blue circle

ridiculous bumblebee
zipping in a web of light and cloud.

May this drunken spin in space
never cease to amaze
wonder, awe,
this rainbow ride,
miraculous height,
galaxy spin, dizzying air
from blackened North America
to dawn gold over pole islands
after sheer space
with only stars and sea below!

Hermes

Ice burns polar
light on these
windows in space.
We fly north over
Baffin Island to
the far point of
Earth's night.

From morning through night
into morning of the same day.

Here we come to what
is real, losing ourselves
in the true confusion
of time reversed.
It is possible to move
into the past, but
not one's own past,
which instead continually
moves forward.

Outside the window are
silver wings—and a face,
Hermes the Trickster,
who sails in space
holding us tight in his arms,

tightly, tightly, until
we finally look in his eyes
and see the full bafflement
of our own faces.

Then he drops us gently
into the ocean cauldron
where the lead of patience
combines with the heat
of our passion, and his own
mercurial blood streaks through
our wound to work the very gold
we knew we could never become
but God made us to be.

Inanna in Hell

Woman hanging upside down on a Tree
in the place of the Dead.

Cold.
Have not been
warm since skin last
saw sun eight months ago.

So this is what it is
to be dead.

I began nearly alive,
the great drop down
into this stinking belly.
No air here.
Stripped by sevens,
seven times standing
nearer naked before
the Eye.

Before I could speak
the Eye uttered Death
and made me a corpse.

Now I hang
upside down and rot
and no bird comes
to feast on my bones.
All wasted.
Lost.

So this.
It does not feel
to be dead.
It only is (not).

The smell of my old selves
wafts through the air like
a spell, a memory, dimly.
Not even the sublime discomfort
of sensing my decay.

When death rots away
will life fall again
from the Tree,
my body find form
in fruit fertilized
by my disappearance
into its ripe wood?
Pray it be so.
Pray this nothing is not
for nothing.
Pray for what I may be.

Destiny

Leap into the Unknown
as quietly as opening
a door or turning
on a light, as easily
as kissing your spouse
Goodbye in the morning
or Goodnight before sleep,
as simply as heating
soup on the stove
or spreading butter on toast,
as needfully as work
in the garden or feeding
the horses, as casually
as washing the body.

In the midst of the ordinary
comes the Moment of true destiny,
without fanfare and with only
hidden preparation comes
the unnoticed moment of passage
into Meaning, in the heart
of the Everyday come our most
dramatic goodbyes and life-making hellos,
in the all-important Everyday
when the ordinary turns into a call
to leap like a sky-diver standing

suddenly alone at the open door
of the plane—without prior experience
and with no assurance that the parachute
will open or of how to find the cord,
but willing to fall free and fly,
trusting totally that the sky
will catch and carry you—and see,
far, far below, the extraordinary
Lamb of God lying in the pasture, or
in the form of a young white seal
with wide-staring eyes, patiently
floating alone out at sea on a solitary
ice floe—and see, then, far out at sea,
your former self, and remember, somewhere
in space, who you are, and that you know how
to swim.

Out from the Islands off North Carolina

To name a place so dangerous
Diamond Shoals, due to the sharpness
perhaps? Or due to the blinding?
Fishermen call it graveyard
of the Atlantic.

Respite in Oregon Inlet
where this east ocean dresses up
in wild wind and pretends itself
Pacific, I see it then,
the treasures, the lure of fish
for men, the mad seduction:

My ocean! My wild gypsy ocean!
That Siren sound, salt bite of sea
that make my nostrils twitch!

A loud wave inside me,
a yell in the blood
that remembers its origins,
the boneshells sick with deadly
longing to go home, Yes!
An invisible body leaps beside me
rushing out to the foam and forever
away—

In the Name of
the Bee & the Bear & the Butterfly

In the beginning, Bee.
Bee of fertility, blessing of flowers,
high priest of pollination.
Bee of My Lady's dreaming,
dressing her eyes, ears, lips, and feet
with golden honey, feeding her
with goddess food for holy milking.

Bee, Bee, lighting on her lotus hands,
kissing her lovely toes with your silken lashes,
leaving streaks of bronze and gold,
powder on your feet from her blue mantle.
Bee, beloved pet, Angel Bee, beckoner,
messenger, bestower, wonder
of the Mother of God.

   O Bee, holy Bee:
   be with us and feed us
   with high-potent sweetness
   and when we grow dead
   sting us alive.

In the beginning also, the Bear.
Great Mother Bear birthing us
in your own image, you teach us

the bearness of life, unbearable
breathtaking bearness of you.
We, in your likeness, learn to survive,
learn to suckle in your furry bosom,
learn to choose within the forest
food to make us grow, growling and humming,
into the fullness of your stature;
learn to labor hard, to fight when needed,
to care for and be cared for,
to rest deep and play well
with you and one another—
we your children,
we your fierce and foolish
tender cubs.

Bear, Bear, you give us teeth and claws
and make us strong with your vigor,
watch over us desiring our self-sufficiency
in healthy measure:
"Bear, I lose my way,
Bear, I fall entangled,
Bear, I feel afraid…
Food you give me of your self,
milk of your honey-feeding body,
berries colored of your blood.
Not only do I drink and chew—
Often, with the teeth you gave me,

I bite you, God."

    O Bear, Great Bear,
    make us your pride and joy.

And of the Butterfly.
Born of life's ending,
promised from the beginning.
All the age-old cocooning,
all the enduring of unendurable happenings,
through long beginnings and endless middle
of our worm-shaped selves:
the unborn butterfly clinging to the bark,
an ugly small worm of a thing made tight,
having no way of knowing, no way of telling
from the tree or sky hope of any change to come.

But by simply being
a good and faithful worm,
allowing itself to die,
surprise! breaks forth
the strangest bird
from its soft, odd-shaped egg,
from graygreen into gold.
orange, yellow, blue, vermilion,
amazing lightness and freedom
with singing wings most Christly,
slipping so lightly and so largely
into the membrane of our souls
through crevices only God can know,
filling all the soft cocoon stretching
spaces of our human hearts.

    Butterfly, brave Butterfly,
    down the wormlike days
    of all our discouragement,

give us the courage to open,
to turn into the unimaginable,
take color, unfold, make music and fly!

Sometimes I Feel the Sky

Sometimes I feel the sky
bending down over my body
and then suddenly a cry
of wild swans eerily
out of the deep silence
of night, in dreamflight
when the world sleeps
its sorrows down,

and on the ridge
from among the fir trees
the silver howling
of coyote or wolf
going on for long
antiphonal moments
together, the wild songs
of heaven and earth.

I feel the arousal
of ancient millennia
of longing, the four thousand
years of advent's yearning
for Birth. I leap up,
throw open the door, step
over the threshold
into that wonderful wail,

invite myself to participate,
all ears, in the souldeep sound,

Then settle in again
to wait in sleep
for the great return,
the pre-dawn birth
of the dream
that will create
a future and change
everything,
the earthquake
in my bed.

Shaking

for William Stafford

There was an earthquake
here the day you died.
Both of you shaking
loose at the same time,
Earth and your spirit.

All summer we loved you,
feted you, praised you.
Too much, maybe, for such
a modest man.

You made us laugh
at everything less than
generous and gracious
in ourselves, and so
you made us be better
than we were or knew
we could be, because
your humility demanded
it of us.

Now it's the end
of August and you,
at home in the afternoon

with a smile on your face,
outgrew your own heart.

A fault opened,
your mortal kinship
with all life revealed,
the Earth shook
you out of yourself
one more time.

The same fault that turned
St. Benedict around last Spring
at Mt. Angel Abbey, but this time,
it turned you.

Before your time stopped
being August, you blinked,
shook free, and flew.

Did you feel Earth dancing
under you, did you begin
to sing the Shaker hymn
that was your life,
your poetry, your work?

> "Tis the gift to be simple,
> 'tis the gift to be free,
> 'tis the gift to come down
> where we ought to be, and when
> we find ourselves in the place
> just right, 'twill be in the valley
> of love and delight."

In Fields of Blue Lupine

In fields of fern
and blue lupine
a silver fox stretches
under the blackberry bush.
There are small cities there,
an arboretum for whole
populations.

A fitting place
for this grown child
of parents who were
children of the Great
Depression and Russian
Revolution—the double
child abuse of poverty
and war.

They taught me not
to live by deprivation
but rather share
exquisitely any bounty
offered me. Indeed, what lack
can there be when one is
surrounded by fields of blue
lupine where white foxglove
spires stretch toward heaven?

Just the Right Tilt

On a planet with
just the right tilt
of 23.5 degrees,
there is infinite
possibility for
variation.

On a planet where ice
floats, life sleeps
in winter to live
another spring.

Dancing in a young
universe, stars still
bump into each other
and star parts into us,
and the night sky
has not yet filled
with unbearable
light.

We can be entertained
by the flicker of humming
alive galaxies nearby.

On this planet of changing
seasons we wobble along
in amazement, awkward
and graceful at once,
with just the right tilt

for the yellow goldfinch
to bathe between the yellow
iris and the yellow rose,
while iridescent emerald
hummingbird sips tea
from hot pink cosmos,
and in me, carbon,
hydrogen and oxygen
hum forth this poem
to you.

A Surprising Species

Deep evening
savoring May
light lingering
over sleeping
trees.
Walking home
I observe
single stars
unveiling
their bodyfires
above a last
ruby streak of sky
low on the horizon,
then eyes follow
the lines of Earth,
single lights
unveiling
here and there
from invisible
houses.
My heart goes out
to them, members
of my phylum,
like fireflies,

a surprising species
that seems to harness
the stars.

Part Two

Burning Bush

Lost and Found

asleep in afternoon
outside in a wicker
lounge
I want to make
music
in my dream,
want to play
the forgotten
sonata,
struggle
to remember
the essential
pattern—
fail, and waken startled
to the western bluebird
serenading Mother Wind
sitting eager and attentive
in my rocking chair.

Volcano

You blow yourself up
to nurture your children,
to draw attention

to a larger reality
than human history,
to teach us

that destruction is
part of creation,
to remind us

that the Earth is alive
and every day of bearable
light is a gift.

The Elements Are in Charge

We live in
a place where
only the elements
are really
in charge,

and we are
all subject
to change,
and

the truth is,
we are in need
of comfort.

Burning Bush

Ascend the high regions
of the body, seek out
its mystery steadfastly,
become prophet in your own
desert, enter the narrow
vault and refine your sight
to its shimmering darkness.

Ride out the corpus callosum,
dark red against gray,
riverborne, cross over, enter
the sparkling cave downward,
descend to the blood source,
marrowstone.

It floods over itself,
darkly radiant, blinding.

Tell no one.
Bow low, humble yourself
before the burning bush
at the center where
brainsteam hums, ganglia
enter and extend—
flames shot forth in longing
to transform each thought

with fire no light or darkness
dare extinguish.

Here, deep and hidden
like a dear danger
within you,
speaks God.

Arctic Quest

for Barry Lopez

Go north as far
as you can.
This means the future.

Go to where summer
is a long day long.
Seek the infinite night.

Go to the lair
of the snowy owl,
the horned lark
and tundra gull.

Practice bowing
to the birds
in greeting
as they guard
their vulnerable
families—eggs,
luminous and fragile
with forgiving life.

Go to where
the white sea lion
and polar bear play

on ice kettles
their haunting chant
too deep for song.

Go to the last thicket
where the sun's eclipse
lures the arctic hare
to a lunatic frenzy.

Go where the map of dreams
takes you, and come back
only when you have learned
how to be one of them,
a true hero, a child of God.

The Blackbird's Child

1

Speeding Life

The Sephardic mandala
on the table in fuchsia,
green, purple and gold—
a gift from Israel, Morrocan
icon gleaned from an artist's
past laid down.

In the middle,
the rose called
Sunfire trembles,
transcending paper,
dimension, the possible.

A mountain rests
on a cloud. This is
the logogram of things:
life, love, evil, ecstasy,
davar.

2

Blackbird

For shabbat I have
scrubbed rocks to their origin:
bloodstone, white quartz
veined with amethyst,
obsidian, petrified
wood.

Fresh water for the birds.
Cut coral bells for
the Shekinah's
companion.

Pale green candles
dipped in the well.
The electric waterfall
of the rock pond—on.

Over this in the bowl
of heaven, The Mountain,
glacial, volcanic,
rose-tinted icefields,
the white breast of Earth,
palatial, impossible.

A hawk chased and tormented
by two red-winged blackbirds.

Around, all around the Mountain.
At the bottom of the bowl of sky
I rest, ready.

The blackbird's child,
mottled, unlovely,
insists at my window,
feed me! feed me!
supper—buttered, honeyed—
koogle for the infant
whose demanding shriek
will lead to a bell,
the sound of running water
in an angel's throat,
what I believe
of the future
from where I sit
with the past.

Twilight.
Moonrise.
On the ground
a large white feather,
pristine,
perfectly Earth and Air,
complete with down,
From where?
This is the country.
This is hawk and blackbird land.

Which one has shed
some hidden underside
of itself?
Are there doves here?

Sabbath Light

1

White and yellow
chrysanthemums
at the window.
Sabbath candles
glowing red
upon the table.
Beyond, the neighbor
boy has climbed
to the roof
of his barn—
a bright red triangle,
confused configuration
like a glowing chimney
suddenly perched
over the manger.
The old horse
takes supper.
The boy waves
at the sun.
He stands at the apex,
his red pants and white
shirt illuminated
in last light, flaming.

The sabbath candle burns out.
The horse stretches in sky.
The boy and the sun go down.

2

In the dark
the kettle growls
over dark red coils.
Midnight tea—
chamomile, for sleep.
And the kitchen light
calls forth winged
creatures of the night.
Pressed against glass
giving itself as
to precious crystal,
the insistent body,
brown and long
between brilliant red wings,
jewelled turquoise eyes,
hovering, orgasmic
in the palatial orb
of Earth, Shekinah,
making love with light.

Not an Ordinary Craziness but Reality

Awakened by this poem
I have decided to tell you

There are spaces between atoms
And my neighbor the scientist

Wears snowshoes in his living room
To keep from falling through them

No Such Thing

No such thing as empty space
No such thing as solid matter
No such thing as one time

    Space is curved
    Matter is motion
    Here is possible
    Now is all

The yellow canoe all by itself
Without being moved is moving itself
Faster than the white rapids around it

The red velvet couch I lie on
Moves a million times faster than my thoughts

My own body and yours moving so fast
Our faces cannot keep up

Which is why they—the faces—wrinkle first
In no -time—so the skin can get closer to itself

Brown Dwarf

So you're small
and solid.
So your solar energy
turned to substance.
So you grew into
form, compact, defined.
So your radiance mostly
returns to make matter
of your own new body.
That's no reason
to call you a "failed star"!
Who do they think they are—
those human wizards declaring
cosmic judgment on you?
How human of them
to consider your particular
miraculous birth in terms
of failure or success.
And what might they think
of our own dear mother, Earth,
a planet in her wisdom
and no star?
But more amazing!
To have made cantaloupe
(not failed honeydew!),
birds of paradise

(not failed pelicans!),
and us–not failed gods.

Affectionate gratitude.
The only right response
to this.
To cherish the unknowable
spectacular gift.
As with the human soul,
so with the soul of any being:
praise words nurture growth.

Go ! brave planet to be!
Are you someone's home
in the making,
cradle of life in the rough?
Let's see all
you can become,
bold young one, child
of the stars—something
new in creation.
In your own being a star
gone solid and not stardust—
Like us—certain life
may come of you.
You may invent a whole new
range of delight for the Universe.
Meanwhile, our species can refrain
from comment, relearn amazement, watch
and patiently wait on the possible.

Ten Things I Do Not Understand

How the telephone
gives me the voice
of my beloved, or
bad news, or gossip.

How the electric stove
makes the egg edible,
or water for tea,
at the touch of my finger
on one button.

How a camera
captures the soul
of a thing—
of course, the aborigines
were right about it.

How it can snow
and still not be
very cold.

Where light goes
in the darkness.

Where books of made-up-worlds
come from in the author's brain.

How language is.

What goes on
inside the body.

Most everything
about myself
and someone else.

That's ten, it's a start.
Ten makes a minion.
I'm ready to talk to You, God.

The Way Things Are

Who's in charge here?
Not us!
Imagine deluding ourselves
into a dominant role—

It's the mitochondria & chloroplasts
who've organized us, their offspring,
into whole societies—they keep us
running & we serve.

We don't need to search out
space for company or kin.
Just look inside your nose
or pick a toe! or the root of a rose!
One eyelash is a colony
of worthy guests.

Understanding this in the presence
of the crab apple tree I do
a little dance to celebrate
the true state of things:
Hallelujah! I'm a neighborhood!

Greening Game

To Michael Murphy, author of *Golf in the Kingdom*,
and Hildegard of Bingen, author of *Knowing*.

1

Satori on the links,
yoga for the mind,
where things are joined
by the deeper self
in the body
as radiance.

2

Viriditas—the mystic's
listening eye, the livening
task of greening, becoming
one with alive green creation,
in harmony with heartstreams,
the greening power of
compassionate love.

3

Trees, grasses, flowing
waters all call me, and
slowing to listen
to their still speech
I see the way clear.

Enthralled by the infinite
colors of things, I go
as my green kin grow,
taking my own sweet time.

A Gathering of Poets at the Lan Ting Pavillion in 353 C.E.

A mountain made of words:
squat men in bunches
scattered on safe paths below,
sculpted under shade trees
in carved crevices.
Will no one in the future
notice none of them is even
pretending to advance upward?

Truly made of jade
the light green mass
looks warm and inviting
and none of us knows
how cold and awful
it probably was,
a serene falsity,
or why the little men
look so embarrassed and pale,
grimacing on rocks,
hiding in conversation
the fact that they are
too thin-souled for the climb.

Literary Ecology

Read poetry—
    Save a tree.

Owl

I have read all
the poetry in
Milkweed Chronicle,
the eastern gardener,
the midwestern farmer,
the northern pole star,
have read all the poetry
in the world tonight
toward dawn to keep
awake, to keep from
my own dark poetry,
to keep all dreams
at bay.

I trust myself
to dream only
by day…

Before light
I surrender.
Let the hunt begin.
I await your will,
Innermost Archer.

Let sleep sing me
a new body,

let dawn paint me
a true lullaby.

Turn

Haunted midway
by the Angel of Death,
divided in duty, too much
attention to the dying,
to seasons of loss,

I seek to be
in one place
and one person,
my place and my self,
to work in the garden
and drink morning tea
where sun rises over
the Mountain.

From there I can live
toward peace.

There I can move
toward a better world.

There I can find
room for my desire
and not be destroyed,

room to breathe
while I wait
for the stars.

At the End of this Road

The dream says wait
by not-waiting.
Enter fog fully,
give yourself
to the cloud
completely.

Go to the white summit
and then turn around,
not to go back but
to see the other side
of your self and the whole
path by which you brought
yourself here. Then hold
to the Mountain. Stay
until morning.

Drink what warmth
the dazzling gives.
Eat light like a leaf
and be transfigured.

Learn all the secrets
the snowy desert
can teach you in one
incarnation.

Do not think you are
waiting for another part
of your life to begin.

Be intrigued. Be overwhelmed
where you are, taking time
to note how everything comes to
you unbidden to meet your desire.

Cultivate not waiting.
Learn the new speech
that thin air makes.

Where you are is
nearly over and
is always. Wait
without waiting.

White Train

In the winter months a white train, heavily guarded, carries nuclear weapons and parts from Texas to Washington, meeting citizens for peace along the way…

White train, you poison Earth
and wail your eerie cry in the night,
snake your death shuttle in shame.

White Western Dragon,
you carry our sins.

Over living bodies
you persist,
a winding wall,
while guns protrude
from windows to guard
your volatile load.

You are white,
the color of ghosts,
the color of grief,
the color of dread.

But in our dreams,
anguished dragon,

you are on fire.
In our dreams
you burn blood red.

Plumed Serpent

Into the well
they threw
their treasures,
these Mayans—

jeweled emblems,
God masks in
rose gold,
copper flagons,
and their children,
some excluding heart.

"They will live forever"
with the gods of under-
ground.

The heartened ones
climbed out
secretly after
dark and began
their own
corn crops miles
away, an offering
of thanksgiving.

Hundreds of years
the daily need
for rain
prevailed.

One year
far in the north,
ten thousand caribou
drowned crossing
a swollen river
during winter migration.

That same year
the plumed serpent
hurled down the corner
of the Temple Pyramid
throwing diamonds in shadow
at the moment of spring
equinox—a new reckoning.

And three Russian cosmonauts
returned from a summer in space,
gently circling the sky
in a giant balloon, delirious
on air, breathless, heroic,
shining like gold, clinging
gratefully to the warm rock of home
as Earth took them again
in Her heavy embrace.

Taquitz

At the foot of the mountain
on the desert floor
there is a shrine
to the god who eats people.

Monster god,
guardian of the desert,
mountain master,
holy terror.

The god wears masks
and lures young braves
up the face of the mountain,
lures young wolves from the canyon,
lures young women to explore
the rocky sinews of their lover-god.

Once in a generation one comes,
woman warrior or cat-footed man,
who succeeds, who survives, who rides
the back of the god laughing
all the way to the top.
These ones tame Taquitz,
these ones mate with the god,
the god in her glory,
the god in his need.

When the mad god is tamed and married
those who live near the mountain
rename it Lily, for wedding blessing.

For the Sacred Marriage Feast
the desert rains come and flowers
bloom through brown earth below,
the mountains close their pain
and smoke ceases for a thousand years.

Everyone is happy, happy,
that the god is tamed.
Happy, happy the god
is wedded and bedded
for a season of peace.
How had the god longed
for a match, longed for a mate!

One who would not believe
in the terrible and laughable power
of the god-who eats-people,
one whose own power to climb rocks
and reach heaven, bloody and broken,
gave joy to this god,
joy to the climber, joy to all creatures.

Blessed are all things
when once in a generation
someone defies, denies the right
of the terrified god-who-eats-people,

when once in a generation
a being forfeits faith in the right
and power of the masked and frightened god,
when once in a generation a being rises
who can love the god from death to peace.

The Wood that Hides

Black Buddha the size
of a jewel she wears
around her neck between
her throat and her heart,
encased in sterling silver—
a gift from hiding.

He made it for her at night
when the revolutionary meetings
were over, the secret leader
of the movement to return,
the people's hope on the border.
He moved around undetected,
disguised, and alone in the dark
with no windows, by kerosene lamp
he carved the holy figure
from the heart of the tree,
the sacred core, the wood that hides.

In ruins of Angkor Wat trees grow
where altars stood; their sap
smells of incense, their leaves
burn like stars in the dark.
There, traveling on foot and hiding,
he rested once in the hollow
of a felled grandfather tree.

A great wind must have taken it
by the root. You could see
in summer light through the stones
where once the sky came down
as Fire and scorched the living
creature, when its spirit was yet
young and able to grow again,
a sacred thickness deepening outward.

Now he rested there,
a solitary aging man
in the dead arms
of an ancient tree,
turning itself into
altar stone.

He took heartwood from the place
his sleeping head had warmed.
He gave it the shape of the Enlightened one.
Its flesh was blacker than black,
carbon pure, luminous.
This he gave to the first woman
who offered him compassion
in his exile. She wears it
always under her clothes,
like a piece of his bone
on her bone.

Cosmic Eye-con

The Mountain is an Eye
inverted, framed in blue,
the pure white iris
opening wide on a world
of stone, lashed on
three sides by fir
trees, closed by
a blanket of bone.

Rachmaninoff Weather

Intemperate beauty
in a temperate place.

Sudden unreasoned change.
Constant.

Clouding of mountains,
rain-rapture weather.

Now weep for beauty hidden
or admire the veil.

The Legend

1

I came burning
away by autumn
on Route 26

traveled by log-rolling
road on the brink of morning,
bright seal-eye of day,
through sloping pine forest,
new growth of the twenty year
timber burn.

Ten minute bus stop
by cow smell of purest
earth the other side
of a turning butte:

Vernonia in September
hints of snow, town sleeps,
rust, vermilion, one black-
eyed cloud on the burnt-
out mountain.

Two stores and a gas pump,
stump sticks and fern red,
moss brown rock stream.

Here an ancient dead volcano
flattened in glacial love,
here men crouch naturally
in tall canyon's shadow.

The rockland verdant bed
by yieldless sea-going trail
points westward.

2

Arch Cape thunder crazed
says Welcome on surf's edge
after ten days' trip from
the city's bowel.

At the moist-filled coast
rain gathers cradled in valley cover,
sits light between rock cliff arms,
erect young mountains.

3

Screeching warring storm-sickened gulls
circle carrion caw on foodless sand, waiting.
A steel white line thin on ocean's edge
from the Orient, jasper sky on the first evening.
I watch the heaving waters rise, bow to heaven's
    weight,
move out of fog Hay Stack Rock, then south old
Needle Point moving in indefinite dusk, seeming
mast-like as a spectral ship appearing now
    disappearing,
spirit-ridden.

Ahoy!

Optic prism on Tillamook Rock at Ecola's foot
one mile out to sea lights up on the clear
sunset evening late as the watery horizon swells
to breaking, releases unknown secrets, belches
them on foam as the mystic purple-white goose
    chases
the lighthouse keeper into the sea at death's flicker.

Giant phantom birds' mammoth voices scree all
    night
on winter ice, the bodiless carvel ship appearing
to northeast: Breeches Buoy and cargo net left
by running Manzanita Tender's tender boom,

burning beacon
gleams on two-hundred foot high island.

Above the woodland promontory lie still expectant
eyeswide deer, elk, bear, cougar.

In dawn gray Lupatia's sunken wreck seems gone:
dog, captain, crew rise in formal line,
the bland Ahoy! Again Ahoy! heard
in coastal villages only the mizzen top mast
jutting aflame, lightning downed.

Here black dragons sleep, waken at night
from three undersea volcanoes' bellies—
ghost men pull their tails.

Abalone, sand dollar on shimmering sand
wet from storm's night.
Hiding in a cindering log watching
the lighthouse wondering, then chasing
pudgy speckled gulls, I trace myself
on sand, am washed to sea at low tide,
forgotten, secret, spectral as the strange
tracks of squat sea birds I followed here
as nowhere I ever was in all my life.

Winter Dream

Inside the body
there is an outbreak,
the skin struggles
to release the cries
of a lifetime locked
in other people's dreams.

As the gray day dissolves
into night I let winter
close round me like sleep.

In the glistening black
my dream descends:

The birch tree after an ice storm
encased in crystal!
How can it breathe?

Perhaps then
it breathes
only light…

Something's bolted!
A horse set free
by lightning,

gate-crashing
life's party,
set on fire
by flying cinders,
hair aflame,
the afterglow
of ecstasy,
melting,
melting
ice where
the hoofprints
go.

Round and round the tree
the horse cries, leaping
over frozen limbs, displaying
teeth, eyeswide, no carousel
dancer, dying to live.

In their startling mating
dance, tree and beast entwine,
melting, melting, and boughs
weep longingly.

Come, waters
that cannot quench
love but do quench
death, pour out all
your passion of tears
as if you had been alone
and in love forever.
The mane is quieted.

In subsided agony
the head leans
against the bark.

Both freed, amazed
in each other's sight.

    Put no house here,
    no barns or buildings
    of any kind.

    Let the grass grow wild.
    Cut nothing.

    So I bless and waken
    from the place, from fire
    and ice, beast and tree,
    and know that I am
    not my former self.
    I never was.

The Cutting

for an Osceola Street Elm

The tree's neighbors stood
to protest silently, to bear
the falling, to bear
witness to the falling,
to bid farewell.

Last night one
at a time
they took the news,
came out from
suppers half-eaten
to hug the creature.

Some trees go unnoticed.
Some trees give joy.

When the cutting began
in the morning
the street became all eyes.

Someone remembered
a tree in Idaho that
killed the man whose
hands cut it down

at Christmastime,
his mother comforted
by another tree
brightly lit
in a dead winter town.

Someone remembered
a rope swing
and six brothers
flying in a tire
in 1933.

Each one remembered
some other tree.

Stroke by stroke
with mechanical ease
the whole tree
and not just its leaves
drawn to Earth this fall.

Why so much sweat
for such a mechanical job?
The houses closed their eyes.

No one breathed.
In minutes
a half-century
cut down.

Ten times the lifetime
of Suzanne's child.

His younger sister stared,
saw the mammoth tree
go down, heard the tree
scream as its body left
itself, severed—

How unwooden the sound,
how alive!

No human voice
but the voice
of the tree.

No blood flowed.
What the tree gave
forth was
cry.

A nuthatch went mad.

Then the child
climbed on its stump
and traveled its circles
of age with tiny feet
and no sound at all,
then stepped down.

But the people on their porches
did not go inside.
They stood to honor
A friend that had died.

Things Get Broken

A child and her father stoop
to pet a dog, vagrant and bold,
nosing his way through commuter traffic
in the station crowd.

Who could say how or who they will turn out
to be, his or her destiny preshaped or cold?

Too much weight at the center.
Nothing holds at the edges.
Nothing holds these days but the sun.

Autumn holds back the hand
about to break a latecomer leaf
that has had itself written on:
"God, why so soon?"

Whistles signal mysteries
and the humble masses acknowledge
their dullness, disperse.

But a weeping man runs after a train,
runs down the train track, waving and weeping.

How an Old Ojibwa Man Became a Priest

for The Rev. George Smith

"Sixty-four years ago
my mother took me with her
to visit friends. I observed.
There she talked always the same story,
the man on the road struck by a flash
as of lightning—a man fell off his horse
in a foreign land and was blind for three days
and kept on seeing the light and waited
till a messenger came to tell him what to do.

"Over and over I heard her talk,
went with her to the priest.
She said, 'One day my son
will be a priest like you.'

"I grew up, forgot in liquor
the promise, the gift I was to have been.
Then the Old Ones sent for me:
'You have been promised to the ministry.
What will you do about it?'

"January 6, Mother sent me into town
for milk. She said, 'Follow the river home.'
The wind changed and I followed the wind.

Cut by snow I stood under the Norway tree
and wept, lost on top of a ridge
and blinded by white, I prayed

*Nin-gah-me-ga-de-wigoney
I will wear the black
if You will get me out of this!*

"An old man became my teacher.
I kept him alive many years.
He taught me not to fear to speak
and made me tell stories to the cracks in the walls
and watch the bridge of his nose.
'I wish I could make you a picture
of what you will be for your people.'

"Now I stand an old Ojibwa man.
I work at Red Lake where conflict comes
in my church, where my wife finds a bullet
in the organ she plays. I talk about Isaiah
and tell them Do Not Be Afraid.
Remember your God with confidence.
I know what I am to my people,
the young ones, Sisters and Brothers,
you are my relatives. For you
I will wear the black. For you
I have gone the way
though I did not know the way. For you
I bless the lightning that comes in snow."

Fire of the Earth

Advent Poem

For the girls who wait tables
in the city every day is a bad day.
The young men come through here
barefooted with too long hair
and rings on their toes.

All the rushing noisy stations,
all the greedy government officials,
the yelling guards who have to organize
strangers who come here for the first time.
Sure enough it's their job.

We have seen strange types
all up and down the market place
these nine years: misery riding
camels, whining children
who will be satisfied with nothing
and tired young mothers.

Something is wrong in the crowd today.
There is even more unrest than usual,
but the people are quiet, their faces
stricken as though they have heard

of some calamity and are fearful
for themselves and their loved ones.

Surely in the last town
they have heard rumors of flood
or earthquake, of tornado perhaps.
But ask someone and no one says anything.
Only silence comes out of their eyes.

Something is surely coming.
Everyone agrees by the hurrying
that something is surely and suddenly coming.
What will the people do?
How will the office clerks get home?
What will become of the sullen young women?

No one's hands are touching.
All the men are cloaked in themselves
and no one is moving with real urgency.
Even the sybillic sky has changed
from gray to ultramarine and purple.

Little fires are started up
in preparation for this night's activity.
My wife and I feel the chill of stillness
coming with the evening.
The people are huddling closer together
as if some desert wind has blown in
pushing them into the firelight's certainty.

Travelers are still pouring through.
Perhaps among them before this night

is over someone will be able to tell us,
someone who has heard in another town,
understood it in the sky or by
the wet unwintery wind,
come to the inn and tell us
if anything is going to happen
and of what we should do.

Gloria

Light wisps low over Earth
at the crying of your birth,
a world cast on the face of night
become bright, bent childlike
beneath winter's feather of a moon.

Tree People

Flicker, how rare
to see you
joining grosbeaks
and pine siskins
at the seedbox,
red-shafted
surprise amidst
a glory of goldfinches
—at my window
a blessing
from the forest
primeval.

Ancient ones
hold counsel—
I can hear them
tree by tree
discussing us,
dangerous visitors,
ignorant in the domain
of green majesty.

Redemption

So many millennia ago
You leapt up
from the bloody tree—
are You not now
weary

of the blood
of Your saints,

longing for them
also to discover
the secret

of the Great Dance?

God Is a Verb

God
is
a
verb

God is one
mighty
roaring
verb

God is
One

God is
Mighty

God is
Roaring

God is
a Verb
roaring

God Is.

This verb named God

we now name New Being
solar lunar sidereal
motion soaring
breathing burning lightning
ultrasonic
SOUND

God is in us
we know,
being new,
stretch, strike, light-
ning soar-sound.

Godlike, sometimes we
just have to
rise up and
ROAR.

Prayer Dance

My bodyprayer
is fleet flame,
candledance,
hymn of praise
to your hidden face.

Easter Bear

Eyes of iridescent bornite
unlike your boreal amber-eyed
kin, your blue-fire gaze
is boundless. You come from
indigo ice caverns below sound.
You learn to sing with the whales.

High priest of the Mother,
you stand alone and at sea,
swim for your life or communion
supper, wed the species
you eat.

White Bear vested in light,
paschal beast, ancestor, living
theaphony of Grace, her power
past might radiates in your
agony: alone!

You cry as eerie loons
or gigantic snow owls cry at night—
watery, freezing sounds.
Your voice reverberates over Earth.
In your being, do you still bear
the primal loneliness of God?

Christ

It happens:
the Creator loves
Creation so much
and finds it so
wonderful that
like a passionate
mother or lover
desire overtakes Her—
She finds a way
to enter it,
to experience it
as completely
as possible,
limitations and all.

Vigil

Get a head start
on the day—
abandon the need
to sleep.

In these precious
hours, silent
and solitary,
sacred vigil keep.

As all great feasts
begin, in soulscape's
eagerness, not with sun,
but moonrise—

Childhood's
high holy days
or wakes of old age,
all shimmer in star-drenched Night.

So might we
the aurora borealis see,
comet tails or Extraterrestrials
hovering in our gardens,
and night-blooming flowers open.

These are the hours,
from Compline to Lauds,
when we create a temple
silo to harvest pain,

Transform despair
into life-giving rain.
As angels work
we reshape the dark,

Breathe soulfire
over day-planted dreams,
wait for the descending
Mystery to waken

In each holy moment,
the miracle,
and simply attend and tend,
stewards of the seed.

Moonbath Conception

Before bed at dawn I visit the stars
and roses together. The silk mimosa
leaves are curled in sleep and
the weeping sequoia nods.

I kiss the silken petals of Intrigue,
Angel Face, Smoke and Sheer Bliss—
from deep coral to plum, even pink
Promise glows silver in moonlight.

An owl sings lullaby and bluegreen
stars wink in some celestial code.
Orion's belt is three laser-cut
diamonds tiered straight over the river.

In a starbath of bliss
in this stillness the river's voice
wafts over fields, bearing water spirits'
symphony down into my pores.
Coyote snores.

On the swing I open my gown
and let moonbeams kiss my breasts.
Then in the southeastern sky
over high cedar boughs, Aphrodite's
planet comes sailing upward—

a heavenly bird shines forth,
shimmering body of whitegold.
Bright ruby heart throbbing
in time, wings feathering
sapphire arcs in the waning
nightsky—a starangel appears
and I whisper a known name
in the cherishing dark: *Gabriel.*

Celebration

Not within alone,
not without alone,
not either/or,
here or there,
but both
within, without,
and all.

The divinely Loving One
lives within you, radiant
in the temple of your heart,
resting at your inner hearth,
your body's core, and the fire
that flows through your vessels
is divine, and all your vessels
holy, and your openings and closings
also holy.

And the warmth created in your blood
is the same warmth as the golden sun
gives forth, flooding Earth with light and life.
And so the stars are temples also, and all
rivers and seas and tiny, invisible animals
and every plant and tree, also a temple.

And the Loving One wakes and moves,
dreams and dances in the spaces
around each atom, and flies the electric
hoops that give each one its name.

And in each atom's center is
the Holy One's bed, and also beyond.

We—you and I and stars and seas—are
fruit of the Holy One's passion,
our limbs and laughter, light and air
and our darkness, ice and fire—all
longed and loved into being by God's deep desire.

Within you, within me, lies a godling seed,
fed by our love toward its birthing.
And in that emerging will be great gentleness
and grace—pleasure and yearning delight,
and Creator/Creation in full-filling embrace.
For God is Both and All,
within and beyond,
O! Most Intimate Mystery!
In you and in me,
in the rock and the tree,
and in all the spaces
between.

Music

Visiting the garden I listen
to dahlias and roses murmuring
and singing among themselves—
Coral Gypsy, the wind dancer,
proud Gay Princess, intense Joyride,
delicate Silhouette, soothing Moonglow,
regal Heirloom, Promise, and Intrigue.
Scattered around them, rustling
feathers of crow and blue Steller's jay.

Without announcement the sky
whips itself out of champagne
froth into a coral pink orgy,
then sets out a pattern of immense
tonal layers—angels fingerpainting
to polyphony.

I lift my small baton, find
the Baroque fluidity, catch breathless
the nearly-too-rich hues between
forest graced branches, turn notes
with this pen into chords of high praise:
God in heaven thank you
for this heaven on Earth!

Eclipse

Between worlds the harvest
moon comes up into Earth's
fall shadow. Everyone is outside
to watch creation's dance tonight
—new neighbors meet
for the first time this
welcome feast—three
glasses of golden wine we
three women raise to greet
the moon. Dragon's breath rolls
away from the river floor
and we see the river loop and
whole expanse of mountain range,
pools of green pasture and
tree islands open themselves,
boysenberry vines swell
with small tides in each cluster,
our eyes open and stretch with
the sky.

A white shoulder crescent
of angel's wing begins
level with the base of the mountain,
then is pulled up out of horizon mist
into nothingness

until, at the volcano summit,
a cosmic disc lifts our souls.

We rise and bow
to the benediction
of a gigantic Host

resting where three angles
merge mountain with moon.
We are small spectators
turned into sacred attendants
of the Mystery.

In this moment, many births
and deaths we'll learn of later.
In this moment, communion
of all beings moving
to the edge of the world.

Seven Peaches Jar

Mint green—
palest mauve—
peach frost—
porcelain.
The fruit not
peach but almost
crimson—
Listen, they say,
the ancient story
shown by fruit
alone—

The Queen Mother
of the West, Xi Wang-mu,
brought to the Han
emperor Wang-Di
twenty-two hundred
years before,
the gift of seven peaches
of immortality.

Why, then, for abundance'
sake or luck, a blessing
or a boast of divine

Nature's bounty, are there
actually nine peaches
painted on the jar?

My Body the Earth

Grass, sand, rock and earth
for a floor, water for all
that cleans and refreshes;
mountains are altars,
the canopy of sky
our vaulted cathedral's
sound roof, and the planets
and stars are our votive candles.

For me, our Mother the Earth
is the House of God.
Her music and walls are breathing,
alive,
Her rainbows are stained glass windows
that sing.

To live here in this body
is to be summoned to worship,
mindfully be part of the sacred
story.

And when Earth rages and groans
in self-sustenance and birth,
she demands our attention.
She requires our response:
Love, Thanks, and Amen!

Cape Foulweather

Whiskey Hill Bridge
Washes Out Over Pudding River.
Road Closed from Foulweather
to Agate Beach.
Twelve inches of rain
in three days.

Eight year old Amber
drowned in a culvert
going to the mailbox.
Saddle Mountain in the Coast Range
is a river of mud.

Bear Creek, Mission, Squaw
and Buckaroo—all surging
rivers now, and the land itself
writhes like a sea serpent
under siege.

Terrified cows trapped in their pen
are taken by the torrent downstream
to their deaths, and llamas snared
by a fence are left behind.

Seven hundred roads and more
are closed and human's houses break
above the shifting, liquid earth.

The Long Tom River
and twenty-three others
stretch now to merge
with the mother ocean.

This storm's official name
is the Pineapple Express,
waterfalls rushing from Hawaii
to the Mainland's Pacific Northwest,
without sweetness, in a cleansing rage.

Gophers and frogs come to tea
in the amber waters of my living room.
We are in creature mode, disoriented
and scared.

Upriver at Paradise Park,
Rose and her two children
huddle and cry through the night
in their old schoolbus home,
while John Wayne, her husband,
makes tree bridges and the flood
takes them from under his feet.
Finally a boat comes along,
the Zodiac, and rescues them
one by one.

On the reservation the old
and sick refuse to leave
for high ground.
The Indian grandmother explains:

"Winter is when Mother Earth
does her house-cleaning and
washes and blows away the weak
parts of her body, and rearranges
her furniture.

"Best to be mindful
of this and get out of the way.
For those who are ready
to move on into Spirit,
waiting for the Mother's will
is a noble way to go."

And I Walk Among Them

Around here animals
are allowed to be
themselves, at home
utterly in the cradle
of creation.

Come Spring
and the mama cows
walk up into the forest
bordering their pasture
to give birth
under the cedar trees,
and the midwifing birds
sing encouraging songs
to them.

Down the road
and around the bend
at sundown hens
and roosters fly
into the low tree
branches and prepare
for avian dreams.

And I walk among them,
at last an animal

happy in her whole being,
singing and greeting
and blessing and being
blessed and thanking God.

"Do You Live Alone?"

Impossible!
Think of it!
Inside the walls
and joints of my house
are trillions of creatures,
some so small the ant and mouse
and solitary bee seem giants—
not to mention those who cuddle
close for warmth and crumbs
outside—thousands of species
of birds and insects,
rabbits, moles, creepy-crawlers
of all sorts, the neighbors'
cats and dogs and cows and geese
and sheep and horses.

Then inside are
the heavenly hosts
who welcome me to my table,
and earth angels in food and flower,
so open to intimacy and even union
with eye, nose, hand, lips,
organs, words, dreams and poems.

Besides these, all
human colleagues

represented by each object:
the artists, laborers, crafters,
ancestors and friends behind
the presence of every beautiful
or useful or meaningful object
here.

And the forest of trees
that live on as furniture,
picture frames, and the very
structure that is *home*.
I share my tree house
with millions of unmet mates
gratefully.

Mealtime meditation
brings in even more, transient
guests—those myriad beings
who have been part of my food's
journey here.

I neither live alone nor eat alone.
Sometimes I need to step outside
to taste a moment of relative
solitude, and even then
it's an illusion: the stars are
as with me and alive
as the sleeping bugs in the ground
beneath my feet.

I can stretch in any direction
and bless it, knowing a companion

is there within touch.
And because I know that every bush
is a burning bush,
I ask the roses not to burn my lips
when I bend to kiss them.

On Being a Mammal

Strawberry Moon
Wild Rose Moon
to begin and end
this month.

On Marmot Road
the tree I love
asymmetrical
like me opens
its one good arm
in welcome.

The slow suffering
body wants to go back
to Earth before
all the parts
wear out and so
it leans toward her
body deeply
and I do also: I touch
the tree and remember
a thrill of conviviality:
we are both made of the same
double helix molecular
quiver.

Sitting still
on the ground
I become a life ladder—
small birds climb
over me on their way
up or down.
They take me
for the base of the tree.

Soon a red fox yawns
in the berry thicket,
beaver shift themselves
from work to play,
and cows lie down
in the sun, their copper
bodies glimmering peace.
A rabbit sniffs
the evening air
approaching and runs
from day's done
hoofbeats heading
for the barn.

Learning to be myself
from them, I yawn, rest,
sniff and stretch
against the sun, listen
for the honey hunter
to come out of her den
and witness this session
of summer school.

A red dragonfly circles
the red hummingbird
circling a red wildflower.

Nose to nose with a doe,
mammal to mammal we
quietly regard each other.
I tell her how glad I am
to have followed my instincts
here—how doing that more and more
cheers a girl right up.

Sunset moon rises full
and pink over the pink
wild rose and the rose
white mountain cuts a summit
triangle through the middle
of the moon.

We are beings
at the edge of the world.
The world is on the edge
of night. We are called
without exception
to learn more deeply
to love each other.

Easter Gatha

First hummingbird of Spring.
Chickadees court in the cedar trees.
Rhododendron buds break open.
Robin sits on rosepink cherry boughs.
Between branches, robin's egg blue sky.
Goldfinch lights on the Oregold rose.
The air wafting incense of azalea
and apple blossoms, aromatic silk
on the nostrils. I sit in the garden,
orgasms of eye and nose,
multiple orgasms of heart and soul.

Hymn to Gaea

Mother Earth's sweet green fur,
or sun-bleached bones of sand
or red-parched skin of shale,
the children swimming in her blood—
marvelous manatee in gentle hospitality
or shy-singing whale,
coral, starfish and eel,
seahorses, plankton and pearl,
and land angels of elk,
eland, ibex and deer,
giraffe and lion and the beautiful bear,
foxglove, human child, and wonderful wolf,
and into infinity of stars I sing,
and I sing of them all, enthralled,
enraptured in you, Beloved One,
in all your creation,
every molecule a miracle!

Part Three

Eaten by Angels

Colors Derive

Colors derive
from fruit
& flowers—
peach, lilac,
apricot, rose

their names
onomatopoetic
of the colors, odors,
the smell !

Think of others—
trillium, day lily,
harebell

say & taste them
in the utterance,

their succulent
stamens, most
juicy stems,
what profligate
eats flowers
with such names,
such delicious words—

it is the same
as tasting
sunset
with one's eye.

Blessing of the Stew Pot

Blessed be the Creator
and all creative hands
which plant and harvest,
pack and haul and hand
over sustenance—
Blessed be carrot and cow,
potato and mushroom,
tomato and bean,
parsley and peas,
onion and thyme,
garlic and bay leaf,
pepper and water,
marjoram and oil,
and blessed be fire—
and blessed be the enjoyment
of nose and of eye,
and blessed be color—
and blessed be the Creator
for the miracle of red potato,
for the miracle of green bean,
for the miracle of fawn mushrooms,
and blessed be God
for the miracle of earth:
ancestors, grass, bird,
deer and all gone,
wild creatures

whose bodies become
carrots, peas, and wild
flowers, whose bodies
give sustenance
to human hands, whose
agile dance of music
nourishes the ear
and soul of the dog
resting under the stove
and the woman working over
the stove and the geese
out the open window
strolling in the backyard.
And blessed be God
for all, all, all.

Creature Covenant

> "And if the chain of Being goes on, and we are only the end of it because we are blind to anything that is beyond us, then perhaps Plato's Intelligible Realms are filled with those creatures of Pure Mind and Music that used to be called angels...
> Above us in the food chain may be angels, below us may be goblins and fairies."
> **Imaginary Landscape,** William Irwin Thompson

To W.I.T.:

Deep in the anaerobic dark
of my gut, is it fairies
I have eaten, now
having a blast, going out
with a war cry to announce
themselves?

In Fairy Faith, these
ancient wise ones
will let their presence
be known no matter
the form—onion, fungi,
or nut.

Though they be sandwiched
between poetry and cybernetic
truths, their mutable powers
live on and become me.

In innocence I have
devoured my elders,
gobbled goblins,
their wrathful cousins
who shriek gracelessly
at having yielded their world
to us.

I beg their pardon,
make a pact, enter
creature covenant
with those I have eaten:
in me and my deeds,
may your dreams be fulfilled.

If I prove worthy and true
one day in my turn
I may be angel food.

Seeing the Cellist

Seeing the cellist
on television
I want to say
something, not about
their tones, but
look how the flesh
rides her bones,
the might of Titania
matching Oberon
at play,
Hera holding Zeus,

all the power

of a red gallop
around the globe
under her clothes
where diaphanous
sleeves show
the muscle of her arms,
she lifts a galaxy
with one bow,
she holds the music
deep in her lap,

long hair falls
to the string quiver,
her power, *her* music!

Nagwalagwatsi

(Origin of the dance—Kwakiutl story.)

She stumbled into it, unaware
of beaver, lynx, coyote and bear,
unaware of raven, rabbit and mole
whose lair she invaded—
and to festive song,
with glistening eyes
their dancersouls became her,
her kin—uncle, cousin,
sister, aunt, godmother—all
human folk encircling her
waist, arms, hair,
catching her by delight
and surprise catching them
in the Great Cave Dance.

To keep their secret
they let her leave
their power source
with the gift of heaven,
changeling magic,
holy rollick,
how beings move
in thunder and joy
beyond themselves.

Bakerwoman God

Bakerwoman God,
I am your living bread.
Strong, brown Bakerwoman God,
I am your low, soft, and being–
shaped loaf.
I am your rising
bread, well-kneaded
by some divine and knotty
pair of knuckles,
by your warm earth hands.
I am bread well-kneaded.

Put me in fire, Bakerwoman God,
put me in your own bright fire.

I am warm, warm as you from fire.
I am white and gold, soft and hard,
brown and round.
I am so warm from fire.

Break me, Bakerwoman God.
I am broken under your caring Word.
Drop me in your special juice in pieces.
Drop me in your blood.
Drunken me in the great red flood.
Self-giving chalice swallow me.

My skin shines in the divine wine.
My face is cup-covered and I drown.

I fall up
in a red pool
in a gold world
where your warm
sunskin hand
in there to catch
and hold me.
Bakerwoman God,
remake me.

Country Life

The Mothers

Under the eaves behind her bed,
the female bird coos in the dark,
the sensual mother-warble,
the delight on eggs.
Night after night she waits
for the confident flutter
of wings to launch her
flight into dreams.

Dawn explodes with the song
of bees, immense, gentle,
black Solitaires—they rub
their furry backs and bellies
on rhodie leaves, on featherpink
azalea, then descend, dancing
the way entire,
behind her serene head where
she breaks fast in the morning sun,
revel in her lilac gown and
velvet brown hair, sip from her cup,
balance on the rim for a greeting,
a prayer they share in secret pleasure—
then finally dive into the cracks

around her living room windows,
her whole house their blessed nest,
ripe with joy for their young.

The Lovers

A single blackbird stands
near the nose of the bull,
unnoticed. He has eyes only
for The Beloved, she
who stands a whole head taller,
whose passionate pity for
his longing moves his heart.
He follows her, emulating
every move.
They rest in a spoon nest
on their bed of May grass,
the newly orphaned red and white cow,
the newly weaned baby bull
with shaggy gold hair,
grinning in the sweet green of spring,
eager to embrace their peace
in dignity or madness,
Queen and Consort
of this pasture haven.

The Man

The new comer.
Where blackberry brambles grew
wild in weeds on three acres
and swamp prevailed,
he entered retirement
with purchase of land.
He tenders it.
Naked, he moves onto the field,
upturned earth made ready,
he bends to the Mother, lays seed
in her furrows, pats down
her fertile body over Promise.
Dry heat causes him to do this slowly,
taking time to realize
the importance of their bond,
to sing the essential, rising
from his knees.
That night it rains.

The Woman

Born for bliss but thwarted,
she came here to overcome her fear.
Her friends recoiled in normal ways—
from serpents, mice, or men.
Her terror was of cows.

Proximity and study failed her.
At last, in despair, she determined
to end it, her life, a suffocation—
she played out the metaphor.
For reflexive bullets she loaded
a basket with golden apples and wore
her best golden gown for burial.
So armed with her own demise
she entered the herd.

They circled, they nuzzled,
accepting her gift, mistaking it
for generosity or trust.
They licked her with thanks,
they cleansed her of salt,
they drenched her gown,
then rubbed her skin dry
with affection, taking her
body barely between their sides,
sensing fragility.
After an hour she opened her eyes.

That afternoon she served tea
to her husband and children
right against the fence,
smiling on and on, throwing
covert winks across the border
to her kin, those grazing kine
on the other side of creation.
Later, she drove up the hill
in bloom,
to buy more apples.

On Killing a Recluse Spider

Three spiders near my bed this month—
under things, elusive, then darting
rapidly toward my body. You or me,
we're the same—dangerous when frightened,
lethal when successful at defending ourselves.
You could kill my hand, inadvertently
stretching across the sheet—my *writing* hand.
Or destroy my foot, too near you in the dark—
you could kill my dance.
But I hate it that I killed you,
though you would have done the same.
This is war talk, and that's what I hate.
I ruined a new book, *Global Mind Change*,
hitting you. And I ruined my hopes
of peace among the species.
The enlightenment book is battered now
not from reverent use but from killing you,
damn it!

Smug in the diurnal liberation
of house-trapped insects,
at night and in utter vulnerability
it's a different matter.
You wake and roam—you patrol—
where I sleep, weaponless.
Only my habit of insomnia saved me.

I'm sorry. Forgive me.
Move on to a higher life form.
And may you have no family
to avenge your death.

Quail

Earth isn't a safe place—
memories lingering
in brown grass and the oak
leaves will kill you.

But these birds
forfeit their wings,
walk as a tribe
across the frontiers
of my pasture, breach
the electric fence,
avoid trees, graze
among wild flowers
in the flat place
the wild deer made,
resting.

Inside winter windows
I curl into the present,
silent, protesting those
friends who want me
to wear widow's weeds
like wet feathers,
forfeiting the future
for the sake of the past.

I shake out my being
each morning, determined
toward flight.

But I watch them
coming, that little colony
of quail, ignoring neighborhood
dogs, cats, and the vagrant
hawk, refusing flight,
walking, walking, moving their feet
like vines in the earth,
rooted, free.

I remember their ancestors'
bodies on dinner plates
in expensive restaurants,
bathed in sauce, truffles
stuffed under their skin.
Their bones were so small.

Conscientious Objection

the frog appeals
the lizard does not
mail says "meat is murder"
I think not
but do not like
the system.

something quickens.

the bird appeals
the bat does not
the conscience is
selective and fickle—
the butterfly
but not the fly.

in the jungle
the womanlion kills
the womanox to eat
and zebra goes down.

in the country
the human woman
eats the cow

and the quail
coo to her and
run for their lives.

I want, O I want
to nurture my friends
and share our communion

but to *eat* my friends
and *be* their communion—
God, I object

to Your patterns
in our ways.

My Feet Press Flowers

My feet press flowers
back into Earth, unseen
fragility, roots too small
for the fertile eye.

Sweet green breath of trees
and grasses gives sensual
life to me;
under night cover our breaths
chemically conform.

For breakfast, tree eats
my skinned off cells
from Earth, I eat
the fruit of the tree,
give thanks for life
deliciously

on our preciously edible planet.

Dinner at the Alexis Esplanade

Waterfront dusk,
scallops on my plate
resting on spinach
and citron, crisp,
I bite into flesh,
feel the crunch of sand,
envision swallowing
the ancient mountain
whose quartz crystal bones
I am eating,
devouring my ancestors
for an appetizer
to spring lamb,
waiting to become young
by what I eat, becoming
instead a hundred million
years old—suddenly
ecstatic to find
so much more *life*
in me, grateful and so
glad to have lived!

My Place

It is a round, filled-
in place. No graves there,
and nothing grave.
Language spoken there is often
mistaken for a language that is known.
It is a perpetual beginning,
a starting point that holds
and resumes itself each morning.
It is an island place,
with one inhabitant
in a sea of grass and spring.

The place is alive and loving.
It cherishes the presences
belonging to it.
It is, you see, my place.
I gave myself to it
in instant recognition
with purchase of land
five years ago.
Since, it has tended me well,
and held.
My cries and laughter are in
its walls. It stays awake
nights with me, and sleeps
in the morning.

Its doors and colors suit
me perfectly as passages
that reflect my body's.
Each cupboard encloses
and preserves a portion
of my soul.
And all afternoon, mind
climbs along the windowpath
of sun.
It is the house where I was born.

After the Tempest

Between contractions
of these seawalls
in the canal nearest home—

a hard thing to leave
that island.

Even though there
I was saved from shipwreck,

fleeing bad times
at home—true—there's been
a sea change.

Reports have come in
while I was waiting
for tea.

Still, though the island
had become prison,

friendly but stifling
in its way,

what shall I find returning,
old foes of weather and person
gone—

new freedom
or new prison?

It's a chance one takes,
being born.

Revenant

Lavender lilies grow
as tall as me in
my north facing garden.

East, the white mountain
plants itself in my soul's
three windows.

I sit on the living room floor
where my piano will be,
eating dark cherries,
drinking apricot tea.

The orchard and arbor
are nearly dwarfed by summer
rain's torrent of wild flowers
and rapturous weeds. I revel
in tending them without
cultivation.

An eagle circles the meadow
of my back acre at sunset.
The red fox rushes through.

Geese cry in the gloaming.
Lambs wait for the warm

spring night and sleep.
On the knoll under rising moon
the doe leaps with the mare.

I have had to cross
bridges and rocky ridges
on narrow paths and steep slopes
to get here, to come back
from being lost at sea,
against the current, of necessity,
climbing steadily toward home,
back to the Source.

Holding Together

I. Keeping Still, Mountain.

Under billowing mountains of raincloud,
the snowy breast I love, unseen.

I feel you still.
For I am the daughter of water and fire.
Your fiery heart echoes in mine.

My blood dances through your silverblue veins.

My eyes suckle under moving gray blankets.
My mother is a volcano.

II. The Well

Thirty meters deep into earth:
The Source.

Too deep for trout, too dark
for the visible rainbow.

Mermaids, dolphins, the nautilus
play below my front yard.

Western sun bathes their cover.
Around the opening, laughter of trees:

Dogwood, silk, magnolia, maple.

A chair of petrified wood in stone holds
the listener to secrets the rosebuds whisper.

A time for hearing musical colors,
the well-being underground sound.

Attend: through the solar plexus
the Angel rises.

Seasoning

1

Cinnamon-browned earth
gives over—
green birthbed widens
through winter.
Snow light
on silver river.
Spring breaks.

2

Rain cuts down
rose roots
relentlessly
through summer.
Spirit breaks.

Tending

I tend the earth,
pull weeds,
gather leaves,
plant flowers,
prune trees,
ride horses,
visit lambs,
worship mountains,
walk in the sea.
The earth tends me.

August Apples

I remember Avalon,
Isle of Apples,
Lady of the Lake
and her aging Merlin,
the lost time
of love and magic:

watching in noon light
of late August morning
my neighbors, Dutch
in his faded denim
coveralls and cap,
Gladys barefoot
in a red and white smock,
excited near their golden
wedding anniversary
come September—

out from their own
vegetable green garden,
welcomed to harvest
my orchard—

she, only bare legs
apparent and fresh
as her granddaughter's,

standing high
on a branch
in the tree,

he below in bliss,
shaking it
hurricane hard,
as the golden
apples of Aphrodite
rain around them!

Peaches on the Counter

A big basket
of ripening
peaches on the counter

Cinnamon coffee
and Viennese chocolate
for breakfast.

Sun Singer

The sprinkler encircles
a wildflower acre.
Old iris leaves feed
earth under the August mountain.
Rose rock glimmers around
gray snow at ten thousand feet.

Here below in the Fuji pond
four goldfinches bathe distractedly.
Through yellow rosebuds one sees
their bright heads, bobbing
in homage toward one valiant
swallow above them.

Born with too large a heart,
she grew earthbound—thrashes
herself through the pool
to cool rock, climbs over
volcanic thunder eggs,
shakes her finlike wing.

Then the ascent begins.
Six inches up to the first station,
then stops, shivers, observes.
Japanese maple.
Up again to the second rest,

stops, shivers.
The woodshed.
And so through eight rests
of jutting pyramid rock
she mounts the triangle,
miraculous efforts, determined
as water.

The vertical plane now mastered
she stands at the summit,
small bird on a flat ledge stone
at the ninth sacred station.
Here she stays all day,
singing her heart out, blessed,
winning the respect of the garden.

Her parents bring her offerings
of grasses and seed, and on
she sings, this yogini with wings,
victorious that for another day
she has come up alive
and so close to the sun.

Sparrow

Small minnow
lost
in a sea
of leaves.

Fall Quartet

Sun Jeweler

The Sun Jeweler
is chiseling herself
a necklace of amber
from leaves which have
rained on the Earth.

Red

Worlds around
we walk on autumn,
our feet stained
with the blood
of leaves.

Falling

Autumn sun falling
on them, smiling, trembling, the
trees take off their clothes.

Cosmic Child

Worldflesh—my bones
bones of the old
Red Stars.

Windowscape

The moon comes languidly
on its back—
opalescent skypearl,
shimmering, pregnant and
with amniotic radiance,
a penumbra breaking
through quaking dry leaves
and bare thin branches
of November's cherry tree.

All Saints Morning/All Souls Eve

The seasoning
of spirits loosed
braces in a fine
shaking down

the window out
back shows
leaves and snow
blowing down
together

early and late
for this

the window in
shows a woman
writing on china
in fine colors,
umber and amber,
fire orange,
shows a fine woman
writing secrets
in wood: larch,
oak, flowering crab,
Douglas-fir,

word by word
into wood.

Trees fill her kitchen,
old fruit falls,
old leaves leave
in a season
of leaving, falling, mixing,
the going, the coming,
snow in her hair.

Playing with Angels

As a child and at my friend's wedding
I gave my body to snow and made angels.
It was Thanksgiving.

Now in deepest night of the turn
of the year, I see a trillion angels
filling the windowed sky, a blessed spirit
dancing in each snowflake, sparkling
on cherry branches and azalea leaves.

Where roses sleep I sound
the piano keys, unlock music
to play the new year in,
and an angel sings each note.
Dancing from the chandelier
is a winged lavender and gold Gabriel,
floating above the keyboard serenely,
overseeing the chords.
The piano itself bears the name
of this angel of annunciation.

Beauty, creativity, compassion—
these are the forms that angels take.
Any act of kindness brings them,
any act of courage, and all humility.
Once I left a friend sitting on ancient

stones in a bright green forest
where the River Jordan begins.
Returning, I found her wrapped
in another world: "Did you hear
the music, those heavenly voices?"

"Only the leaves and the river
in wind and sunlight, dazzling."

"No, it was more," she said.
We crossed over the river and
I heard it too. I thought of the celestial
cervix of the Queen of Heaven in the coned
dome of the Church of the Annunciation
at Nazareth, giving birth to radiance,
bearing all creation forth in golden light.
My companion thought of Mary
in her son's arms in Paradise.

When we know we cannot create beauty
or strength on our own, we sense them.
They come to us anyway, unseen and unsung,
those color-doused ethereal ones, the Presences.
But in those moments of sheer reality
when we embrace our small powers,
those greater agents of Grace become accessible.
Then in amazed or natural bliss,
our doors of perception open
and we hear the angels sing.

Real Presences—Nightbird

Who is that bird that
sings in its sleep when
darkness is
sure
to eclipse
any trace
of day, say
at three
past midnight?

Insomniac and reading
late, *Real Presences*,
I hear it
rising from some
high tree branch—
it is a lofty
sound that falls
on my heart, a stabbed sweet sound.

I think of Noble fir
or hemlock, an alpine
conifer, and my house
becomes a cave
in mountain rock

where air thins
the forest into a
cloud of stars.

There is no real
sky at night, but a deep
screen of separate fires,
or nothing.

Who is that bird that
sings only once in the aching silence
midway between deepest
night and dawn? A perfect
trill or complex turn
from God-drunk dreams,
its song gouges out
my soul, devastates me
with the old lethal longing
for time-piercing perfection—
Nightbird, do you live really
in the sky somewhere or only
in my own opacity, clear bell
awakening a dream-deprived mind?

Horowitz to Tea

"He has an idiomatic control,
a demonic presence…"

Sit here, Vladimir,
at the piano.
Play the unspeakable
grief, the gargantuan
joy no vessel can contain.
Just play.
The definitive Rachmaninoff
Sonata, Chopin's Premiere
Ballade,
the Twelve Years' Silence,
diminishing travel,
your daughter's madness,
the daughter who died
finally of suicide, Sonia,
whose life you had forgotten—

the night alone after
the lights dimmed and
everyone had gone home
from Carnegie Hall,
you still hearing
the applause, "Welcome back!"

"Two world wars,
a Russian revolution,
three nervous breakdowns—"
and you still managed
to emerge, to walk on
the stage, acknowledge
your audience, and play.

The old pain stopped
in the *sostenuto*
of the hand held
suspended over the last
phrases of *Traumerei*,
the piece you preferred
above all, the eternal,
flightless dream.

October 1, 1984
80th birthday

Freedom

Freedom is death,
being absolute possibility,
unbearable waiting
for the escape
into a new cage
where

freedom as death
will return,
reclaim us,
until we escape
into a new cage
until

freedom as life
lights us
and we can rise
wounded but healed
from our comforting chains.

Banshee

[bean=woman + sith=fairy]
a female spirit who wails
outside a house to warn
that someone within
will die.

This bean grows
at night,
it is very round
and brown and
underground.

If you dig
for it
too soon
you will see
its beautiful
pregnancy
tear down
and collapse
into soil.

Wait.
Let the ripening
come in its own
good time.

This bean comes
up green
and full of earth:
someone's teeth
have been here,
another's heart
and innards.
Look at the bones
around the stem!

This flower's calyx
is black as moon's dark,
and gives no clear
warning for its turn.

Watch out!

This bean is a fierce Host:
it is many, strange, unfriendly—
it feeds promiscuously, nourishes,
protects all who dare touch it
with their tongues;
it is ghost and guest
in the soul; eat it
and know only the Truth.

This house
you have ceased
to live in
but still occupy
belongs to the bean woman

and her kin:
her leavings
are all around
your door
now.

She's come
to claim
her place.

It is another
night.
The moon is
full.
Someone here will die.

Piston's Suite from *The Incredible Flutist*

Long past the age of innocence
some of us still wear feathers
and sequins at midnight and open
our hearts to enchantment again,
past brutalities and cruelty,
past all stupidities
that make me wonder
if God is out of Her mind
to let us go on.
If I were She I would have ended
the human experiment millenia ago,
a sad failure, a bad quirk of Nature:
Not content with the steady effort
of spiritual suicide, our species
in its place as organelle in the One Body
became macrophages autoimmunely
attacking ourselves and the Whole
cosmic Life.

Yet I marvel how You, Mother Creator,
have faith enough in us to let us perdure.

Now the human children in Eastern Europe
lead their elders through art and acts
of awareness to save the planet
from gross sins of pollution,

greed's outrageous assault on Earth.
A Polish child embodies the fate of a flower
poisoned by industry—a precious few begin
to offer a way to restore salvific life
to creation's body, integrity to ourselves:
science and art unite in the holy work.
Fifty thousand parents and children
go to the beaches at summer's end
to clean up our litter.
We are trying to unfowl our nest.
The brave teach peace, channel anger,
practice patience. Our hearts can still be
collectively moved, taken in music's communion,
when a visiting Chinese conductor raises her baton,

a magic wand, we become one ear in the World's Body,
our shared soul lifted with the gift of lyrical laughter
by oboe, bassoon, the animal whistles and hoots,
horns and bells of Piston, Prokofiev—
or brought to tears of delight or despair
by Tchaikovsky, the touch of a single string.
And I begin to understand why God lets us live…

Why I Wear Black

Colors are too limiting—
bold red, shy peach,
a hundred shades of green—
go mostly with themselves
and only a few others.
Black is expansive,
makes others stand out
vividly against it,
black is generous,
undefined, ready,
open to sudden changes
and surprise—it meets
the occasion. Black goes
with everything.

Blackbird

Blackbird falls like new snow
winged as thin as glass
colored red for drinking light,

falls mystery-wise into houseled
basement crêche, perched on sink
and laundry soap, sings.

Wimpled stroke I steal
from piano bench, easel, typer,
careless-like, surprise by wings!

Find eastering there as
Mary within tomb
God's rising mine

from black to wings,
from small to song,
and freeing her, forgiven,
flying heaven to sun-stunned eyes.

The Swan

The swan
is not precocious
oblivious or obnoxious:

neither precocity nor ferocity
leads the creature
(nor its wit)
to bellow out
gales of wind,
but by its bleating & its beating

in the low & widening evening
in its high & whitening leaving

imitating all the other sounding animals
   whales, quails, frogs, & mammals,

it sits a self-satisfied customer & a good example
of How To Travel Light,
quite non-lugubrious
on the lakeside grass, no ice enthusiast,

and prepares itself, calmly, resolutely,
steadfastly (& it takes so long & is so much
trouble is why this bird
goes lastly), for to get all the air,

every centimeter, hooting & a-hollering
out of every bone hollow & wing filament

    till by crook & by shout
    it can fluff itself out
    for the south trip,
    lighter than air, quick.

Up a cloud climb
(making up for lost time)!
And the Big Blast of Hallelujah Chorus in
November
is what we call the Swan Song, heaven-sent.

Crow

The backyard sprinkler
turns
over the new
seeds marking Spring
under the maple tree;

a Sunday shade of sprouting
grasses.

Crow comes to the water-
fall—to the dark bird
powerful as rivers
over rock
to larger beasts.

Water achieves
its opposite,
gentle to terrible, & crow
understands the water, puts itself
in the midst of the awesome gift,
black feathers shimmering
immoderately;

around & around the turn
through shadows, each step
the bird takes a step through

ages of history; by the darkling
rock garden fenced
in Zoroaster's time
to the Golden Age of Pericles,
ages of iron & of bronze;
the bird understands
what the water holds:
from the beginning. Suddenly

it leaves
the trajectory
finding its own
momentum, straight up;
yang into yin, the old tree
is with wing, black
feathers shine in it
& shake like a small
noon sun.

Something More

Not the old gifts
of winter and year's end—
last night's communion
of old wine and flat bread
is not the common meal
we seek this morning…

Tired from late hours
the butterfly of night
comes hungry for light,
finds flame, is consumed
by the morning star.

Consider winter loss.
The candle wavers with cold,
and warmth is gone, but light
remains, more precious than before.

Outside the windows in deep pools
the frozen lakes hold fish below;
even in deep cold beneath the waters,
movement of their play.

We yearn for light and play
below the frost in the dark hours
of our dreams.

Toward dawn the skin of thin ice
shatters into the spring thaw of ourselves,
blood melts into milk, milk into power.

We are the food as we feast upon air;
as God gives, we give, from overflow
or utter emptiness.

Trembling, touching, discerning
the deep deserving of each
minutest creature: we need
only to give up our disbelief
in the gift inside ourselves

to free our flesh into song,
to fly, to fell the night-eclipsing
Daystar chasing at our heels,
sing Grace, greet God
in a green flower.

Requiem and Kaddish

Not a dog.
Black, beautiful fur,
a still-warm shell
of bear lying by
the road.

What were you doing
crossing the highway?
Where was your mother?

This bear was young,
still the milk-eater,
and stranded.

One by one the humans
stop, truck drivers
and people going to work.
Early morning. Fresh accident.
They bend and ask how
did this happen.

Some touch the paws.
Some stand in silent
witness.

A woman going to her first
day on a new job makes
the sign of the cross
over her heart and prays,
"Go easy into your new life
and be blessed."

So our spirits grieve
our species' harm to others—
the mule whipped raw
in the coal mine,
baby elephant crying
for its mother
in a logging camp cage,

birds poisoned by
poisoned insects,
the lonely prisoners
in our homes.

    For all their lives may God be praised.
    For their freedom from the pain we cause
    may God be praised. For the conscious desire
    to change our ways may God be praised.
    For energy to follow through may God be praised.
    For this small bear, the dog of God,
    may God be praised.

Under the Ironwood Tree

Pa Hunt took me down first
to the place where the dead
beaver was rotting, the pungent
smell of divinity and puss
covering all moss and wood.

Sandy brown its fiddle-back tail
spewn like fans on the naked
grass under the ironwood tree,
dry heather, muskrat, a marvelous
pristine experiment.

Between black flies and bramble
weaving together with the wind
and his terrier, Fi-or's Ransom's
Gift of Bucknam
(Earth and I sired
by the same seed)
Wee Bairn Mc'Dont,
redblack and wiery.

A whole Susquehanna delta
cut like lightning through
the river's sleep, the natural
timber waterback's consecrate
industry.

A Dorian Mode in A strident
along the strings of Pennsylvania
Rubicon—last July the Skirmish,
Chemung wives and their surrogate
husbands together barreling a cannon

as the whole estate
of creaturedom rose
and scattered.

Today, quiet April mist,
blur of murmuring,
dazzle of sound
where beaver and muskrat
have been and are gone,
all who ran out on the living.

I remember the carnal joy
of splashing my face
in a small waterfall
adoring the Other
ten years back as a child
swam naked behind chasing
fishes, laughing resonant
praise, came up from ethereal

grey a Maying undine
whose shadow caught
in flaming orange
and sudan.

Gliding away on Indian biers
father, mother, Name of names
and selfhood.

On the ancient rock with fern
where no dam ever was,
where work is a form of pleasure,
shiny fur lurking in light
with urgent teeth.

In the bly and rustic alcove
called time with bare dimension
in mansions under water
and houses built in trees
behind mountains—rapture.

It is not I
but the same
root and russet
as I in Christ-ground
where myth and substance
merge outside of dreams
in pure sensation,
celebrant wisps of
new creation,
Original Grace
at play.

A brilliant coupling—
the rupture and chaos
of time against time.

We were on the way home
from Sheshequin and beaver
for hamburger dinner
when suddenly the abyss
of sky broke into sunbust
red, opened—

later, pieces of sky shrinking
like barbecued charcoal cinders
in your backyard fire.

How Hard for a Mother or Father to Let Go of a Son or Daughter

*So as custom has it every year
on the birthday of each child
the parents make sacrifice and
fast in the Temple.*

The first year the mother offers lace, the father iron
    And they fast one day and leave.

The second year the mother offers wax, the father sand
    And they fast two days and leave.

The third year the mother offers rice, the father copper
    And they fast three days and leave.

The fourth year the mother offers oil, the father wood
    And they fast four days and leave.

The fifth year the mother offers wool, the father ivory
    And they fast five days and leave.

The sixth year the mother offers silk, the father jade
    And they fast six days and leave.

The seventh year the mother offers pearls, the father onyx
    And they fast seven days and leave.

The eighth year the mother offers fur, the father turquoise
    And they fast eight days and leave.

The ninth year the mother offers flowers, the father water
    And they fast nine days and leave.

The tenth year the mother offers china, the father pewter
    And they fast ten days and leave.

The eleventh year the mother offers embroidery, the father leather
    And they fast eleven days and leave.

The twelfth year the mother offers coral, the father crystal
    And they fast twelve days and leave.

The thirteenth year the mother offers amethysts, the father cobalt
    And they fast thirteen days and leave.

The fourteenth year the mother offers garnets, the father marble
    And they fast fourteen days and leave.

The fifteenth year the mother offers emeralds, the father diamonds
    And they fast fifteen days and leave.

The sixteenth year the mother offers salt, the father silver
    And they fast sixteen days and leave.

The seventeenth year the mother offers honey, the father gold
    And they fast seventeen days and leave.

The eighteenth year they offer their child and leave in silence,
First without touching, then holding hands.

Christmas Morning Mass

Iced in for seven days
so far, I read nights
by stars, listen
to Mozart and obscure
Baroque music, prepare
gifts and messages
for neighbors and kin,
feed the birds who
feed me back more.

This morning while I
showered away from the scene,
the ferral cat next door
had been to the feeder
for breakfast.

I found it in disarray
and filling it got fresh
blood on my hands.

Here, inches away
from my breakfast table
through thin transparent
glass, Nature's feast
endures:

This is my Body
This is my Blood

Pleiades' Daughter

>at the Stepping Off Place

I

I was born when my planet
slipped through the shadow
of Taurus, pet bull of the
Mother, sacred to her
cow-shaped shifting.

My ancestors told stories
of coming from the stars—
Seven Sisters in constellation
Pleiades, at the resting heart
of the bull.

Daughters of a god in flight
from rapacious Orion,
a mantle of mercy fell over them
and they became seven white doves
in the heavens.

Their wings vibrate in space
as pure light, their breasts
are white fire.

From them we come—our home
a worn planet in the Pleiades.
Through the dark, healing and
infinite night of space
we shipped out on lightwaves
between islands, bringing
food as manna from the holy
darkness of home.

Now home grows from starseeds
planted in the garden of a new sun.
We live in the intimate nest
of ancient star doves.

Six of our mother stars remain
visible to naked eyes trained
on night. The seventh has disappeared
into another Forever.
Gone into hiding or lost.

My secret blood is sacred.
I know from which star I come.

II

My lover loves the smell of my body,
with a worshipping kiss he loves
to enter its hidden places,

seeking sanctuary. He tastes
the sweet pungent sacrament
of honey and wine that comes
from the caveheart of nature
in me, my lover's shrine
and mine.

I wonder, will he discover,
exploring there where I can
never go in my body,
some strange manifesting of me,
inaccessible, unknown?

The body's mysteries need
tending and care.
When he goes there, he moves
slowly, with care, a primal
astronomer exploring wet
caves in white fire,
approaching in awe the inner
space of the seventh sister,

deeper, swimming in bloodfire
that pools up from infinite
oceans within—then

into the quiet dark
with its secret
holdings, it sacred
desire, into the wild, wild
heart of the sea—

Fantaisie-Impromptu

At midnight, my prime time,
an Angel is telling me
this immense fiction—
"You will travel at last
the Orient Express from Paris
to Istanbul, sleep in Switzerland,
make love in Vienna,
be rich and philanthropic,
live in a big house on the hill
where the top of the world begins
and ends, live twenty more years
and die in the arms of your lover."
Well, which one?
The one I love now and will marry,
the one I love still and was married to,
the lost first love of my wakening,
the blue-eyed poet with the blood disease
who went south to keep warm,
the mulatto priest in Rome,
or the one who drank plum wine with me
and when he put his tongue in my mouth
made poetry?
None of the last four and
both of the others, I'm sure.
And when they hold me in their
mortal and immortal arms

I may be thinking and laughing
about little red poppies
that grow in Galilee
called Blood of the Maccabees,
and about how I walked
barefoot among them alone
in my thirties, humming
"We're Makin' Whoopie"
in the Holy Land.

When Poets Kiss

*Poetry is more akin
to kisses than to food.**

When the poet opened
my lips with his tongue
and entered my mouth
did we,

in that sweet intercourse
of tongues and juices,
in that double dance
of heat and radiance,
did we

come together beyond
words or was it words
themselves wanting
to come inside
each other's bodies?

When the poet
put his loving
tongue inside
my mouth
did he

plant his words
in my soul?
Did he

eat my words
and take them
to heart? Or
did we

merely feast
on flesh,
two passionate
carnivores
in celebration
of what makes poetry
the second great
oral fixation—
after the kiss?

> *Or: chocolate is the fourth type of oral sex; i.e. there's mouth to mouth oral sex, then there's poetry, then there's oral sex, then there's chocolate.*

Three-handed Solitaire

Left to my own resources
I have three choices:

head-work
hand -work
heart-work

    Say, writing a book
    or a letter

    cooking soup for my neighbor

    writing a poem or
    playing the piano

Now *you* guess
which is which!

Hint: of the eight
pure Taoists
who entered Heaven
one was a gardener
and one was a humorist
and one was a scholar—
all the same one!

The other seven
were loving
married people
and parents.
Enough said?

You Angels Who Cluster

*You do not let us
see your face,
though we are wet
from your radiant embrace.*

I awaken from the nightstorms
of ravaged dreams, fall
on my knees in front of the
television—another war
in the holy lands.

And terrorist acts continue
out of displaced hate
in the icy light of day—
the innocents again.
Always, the innocents.

You angels who cluster
in the corners of sickrooms
and who walk with believers
and unbelievers into gas chambers,
you ministering saviors—
I forgive you.

You cannot save, you only salve
those consigned to creaturehood.

I hear you listening.
I hear you longing
to help us.

I know your presence
and your love.
I would rather be me
than you.

What Am I Doing?

Allowing my trick body
finally to slow me down
so I can savor the gifts
of an accidental life.
Is it okay, Holy One,
that I'm just sitting
here enjoying
the occasional sparrow,
effervescent finches,
rainbow of flowers,
light and shadow play
in the pear trees,
horse tails dance
in greengold pastures,
and surrounded by music,
Mozart and the tricolored
blackbird—

not writing letters
in behalf of political
prisoners or even listening
to my neighbors' troubles?

"At last," says God,
"one of my creatures
I don't have to worry

about today! Mazel tov!
Carry on ! Enjoy!"

I've finally opened
God's birthday present
and discovered the true
purpose of life—
to enjoy it!

So from now on
my spiritual practice
will include plenty
of long periods of doing
nothing but giving
God a good time.

Cycles

Late Sunday nights
in a deserted bus depot
a woman between 40 and 60
dressed in black jeans
comes regularly
with her samoyed dog
to meet the buses.
When the last of six
passengers disembarks
she and the dog take off.

Tonight an old man
and woman wait inside
for an early morning
trip to Milwaukee
eating purple plums
together.

The old man smacks,
breathes, then speaks:
"I'll bet these looked real
pretty on the trees."
The old woman answers:
"Your shoes sure got dirty
in the gravel today."

Then only smacking
and breathing, the sound
of plums en route to Milwaukee.

"What is Prayer?"

Prayer is intimacy
with the Great Mystery.
Be every moment
aware of the Presence—
how you are loved!
She takes off Her wings
to heal you, He surrenders
everything for your sake.
At all times in every
hidden, open place
It lives in your deep
soul's core, It moves
in your moving and acts
through your skin
and the skin or bark or shell
of all living beings—forms of angels,
and also of water, rocks, and fire.

So be awake to the life
that is loving you and
sing your prayer, laugh your prayer,
dance your prayer, run
and weep and sweat your prayer,
sleep your prayer, eat your prayer,
paint, sculpt, hammer and read your prayer,
sweep, dig, rake, drive and hoe your prayer,

garden and farm and build and clean your prayer,
wash, iron, vacuum, sew, embroider and pickle
    your prayer,
compute, touch, bend and fold, but never delete
or mutilate your prayer.

Learn and play your prayer,
work and rest your prayer,
fast and feast your prayer,
argue, talk, whisper, listen and shout your prayer,
groan and moan and spit and sneeze your prayer,
swim and hunt and cook your prayer,
digest and become your prayer,
release and recover your prayer,
breathe your prayer,
be your prayer.

Let prayer be your thinking
and thriving, your passionate
living and humble dying
back into Earth and God.
Let prayer be your senses and sex,
your political power, your confusion
and vision for good.
Let teaching tolerance and all childcare be prayer.
Let your mistakes be a prayer, and your unknowing.
Let remorse and forgiveness be prayer.

Make love in every act,
create growth in each intent.
Nature in any form serves
as sanctuary and temple.

Let your bath be an oracle chamber,
every trip anywhere a pilgrimage,
and your dreambed each night
the Holy of Holies.

And so you are praying.
So you do what you be,
and all your being is blessed
and all your life is a prayer.
And all your acts are a blessing.

Index

A Gathering of Poets at the Lan Ting Pavilion in 353 C. E. 151
A Pig's Winter.. 34
A Poem Heard..78
A Second Coming...51
A Surprising Species...124
A Visit Home for Christmas Rites 5
After the Tempest..246
All Saints Morning/All Souls Eve. 263
An Act of Love...63
An Ant..23
And I Walk Among Them 209
Arctic Quest 134
At the End of this Road 157
August Apples..254
Bakerwoman God..230
Banshee..272
Bear Hug..86
Betrayal..28
Biodance..102
Blackbird..278
Blessing of the Stew Pot..223
Brown Dwarf...144
Burning Bush 132

· 315 ·

Cape Foulweather	206
Cat's Act	26
Celebration	198
Chinook	15
Christ	193
Christmas Morning Mass	294
Chrysalis	100
Colors Derive	221
Conscientious Objection	240
Cosmic Eye-con	168
Country Cousins	83
Country Life	232
Coyote	90
Creature Covenant	225
Cross	69
Crow	281
Cycles	309
Destiny	110
Dinner at the Alexis Esplanade	243
Dzoónokwa	65
Easter Bear	192
Easter Gatha	217
Eclipse	201
Fall Quartet	260
Sun Jeweler	260
Falling	260
Red	260
Cosmic Child	261
Fantaisie-Impromptu	299
Fear	43
Fire of the Earth	183
Flying at Sixty Below Zero	104

Freedom	271
From Here	92
Gloria	186
God is a Verb	189
Going Formal	25
Greening Game	149
Hermes	106
Holding Together	250
Homecoming	10
Horowitz to Tea	269
How an Old Ojibwa Man Became a Priest	181
How Can We Survive Our Choices?	21
How Hard for a Mother or Father to Let Go of a Son or Daughter	291
Hunter	71
Hymn to Gaea	218
I Am Your Poem	74
In Fields of Blue Lupine	121
In the Name of the Bee & the Bear & the Butterfly	113
Inanna in Hell	108
Innkeeper	87
Jewels	7
Just the Right Tilt	122
Literary Ecology	152
Lost and Found	129
Medicine Bear	98
Moonbath Conception	196
More Words for William Stafford	76
Music	200
My Body the Earth	205
My Feet Press Flowers	242
My Place	244
My Yoga Teacher	81

Nagwalagwatsi	229
Narwhal	19
New Depth	37
No Such Thing	143
Not an Ordinary Craziness but Reality	142
On Being a Mammal	214
On Killing a Recluse Spider	236
On the Road Again	88
Out from the Islands off North Carolina	112
Owl	153
Oxbow Farm Incident	54
Peaches on the Counter	256
Phaedrus Pool	45
Piscean Moon	14
Piston's Suite from The Incredible Flutist	275
Playing with Angels	265
Pleiades' Daughter	296
Plumed Serpent	161
Prayer Dance	191
Quail	238
Rachmaninoff Weather	169
Real Presences—Night Bird	267
Reconciliation	96
Redemption	188
Requiem and Kaddish	285
Retreat	35
Revenant	248
River Blindness	61
Sabbath Light	140
Salmon Return	16
Sea Flight	105
Seasoning	252

Seeing the Cellist	227
Seven Peaches Jar	203
Shaking	119
Sky Burial	66
Something More	283
Sometimes I Feel the Sky	117
Sparrow	259
Spiral Rest	44
Sun Singer	257
Taquitz	163
Ten Things I Do Not Understand	146
Tending	253
The Amber Bears	84
The Blackbird's Child	136
The Cutting	177
The Elements Are in Charge	131
The Legend	170
The Swan	279
The Way Things Are	148
The Wood that Hides	166
Things Get Broken	180
Three-handed Solitaire	303
Time Traveler	94
Tree People	187
Turn	155
Under the Ironwood Tree	287
Verdi	73
Vigil	194
Volcano	130
Waiting	41
What Am I Doing?	307
What Is It?	68

What We Can Bear	22
When Poets Kiss	301
Where Life Begins	3
White Train	159
Why I Came to the County or Persephone Goes West	38
Why I Wear Black	277
Windowscape	262
Winter Dream	174
Winter Trio	31
Writing in a Foreign Language	9
You Angels Who Cluster	305

Printed in the United States
4122